MW01297808

Seeds of A Spirited Life

Where does wisdom come from? Or maybe not wisdom exactly—that seems too lofty for the deeply grounded living, searching, doubting, and knowing that Meg Barnhouse shares here.

Where, then, does a deep drive to live come from?

It comes, as Meg shows us, from the seeds of our experience, seeds that are part of a cycle so much larger than ourselves. Meg offers us the stories of her life—the everyday and the extraordinary, the painful and the hilarious—and they are so delightful and so telling that this would be enough. But she gives us more than that: She also leads us to recognize that we too can find these seeds of life, of spirit, and of meaning; they are, in fact, already in our hands.

Rev. Nancy Palmer Jones
Senior Minister, First Unitarian Church of San Jose
Co-author with Karin Lin of *Mistakes and Miracles:*
Congregations on the Road to Multiculturalism

Seeds of
A Spirited Life

ॐ

Meg Barnhouse

Westview
Kingston Springs, Tennessee

W E S T V I E W
P.O. Box 605
Kingston Springs, TN 37082
www.publishedbywestview.com

ISBN 978-1-62880-211-5

First edition, October 2020

Cover art by Kiya Heartwood.

Printed in the United States of America on acid free paper.

Contents

Where Do I Start?

I could start this book anywhere. All categories are inexact.

This book is letting me run seeds through my fingers, sorting them as if I were a character in a fairy tale. Of course, the task is impossible. Here are the seeds of what I have learned so far, the seeds who I've been, wandering around my life like I wander my garden, looking at which events and consequences grew from those seeds.

In the same way that the life of a seed is a cycle, I feel my life as overlapping rounds of cycles rather than a chronology. There are many beginnings, many endings. Sometimes my spirit was in bud, sometimes in bloom, sometimes buried in the dark earth wondering what in the world was going on, crowded, then alone. Longing, as everything and everyone does, for warmth and light and enough space to breathe. In my vision of this book, it is made of beautiful seed-embedded papers, laid one over the other in a collage, so you see part of a story in one space, and then you see the same story whole in another place, told with more and different details. It's not going to be perfectly linear, but we will all be all right.

Learning from the Gardens

ॐ

I always wanted a garden. Gardening was not something my family did. Mama did love red geraniums, and she'd plant a pot of them every spring to sit by the front door. No garden was possible at my first house in South Carolina, because it had a steep deeply shaded back yard covered in English ivy. I spent hours pulling vines, uncovering stone steps and a little stone terrace wall. There wasn't enough sun to grow anything but ivy. The next house was the opposite. The backyard was a flat half-acre. I asked for the Martha Stewart gardening book for Christmas and devoured every page with rapt attention. The garden I planned was round, with a walkway in a circle around a central hill of earth.

My friend Kathleen had some Arabian horses. If you wait long enough for it to age, their manure is just what garden soil wants. We shoveled a truckload of fifteen-year-old horse manure to fertilize that garden. My father, the mathematician, was thrilled to be asked how to figure the square footage of a donut-shaped garden, so I'd know how much fertilizer to use. In the raised center I planted blue salvia, which grew up singing a tall purple song. In the outer ring I planted tomatoes and beans, peppers, zinnias and basil. The middle ring was the walkway. I learned over the years that the peppers didn't like to be planted near the beans. I kept chives and garlic in a bed of their own, mint in a big pot so it wouldn't take over the world, and planted a large half-barrel on the back porch with tulips and pansies. In the spring the tulips would come up through the pansies, and the sight made my heart big and happy. I filled the front yard with daffodils rescued from a nearby field where a strip mall was about to be constructed.

I lost that garden and the front yard daffodils in the divorce. Eventually, I moved into a house whose previous owner had been a gardener, a collector of unusual plants. All I did there was take care of what she'd planted. There were no vegetables, but that was okay, since I didn't really like to eat vegetables at that point in my life. Neither did my children. Underneath a large purple smoke tree she'd planted horsetails, a plant so ancient it doesn't even have leaves — just a stem. Dinosaurs would recognize that plant. There were hyacinths, a purple hydrangea with a white rose growing up through the middle of it, and a patch of dwarf purple iris I found by accident one spring as I was weeding behind the butterfly bushes and false indigo. Her garden thrived, and my children and I thrived there too.

A garden feels peaceful to me. It puts change and turmoil into a time frame I can deal with. The earth is on the boil, you know, and rocks from deep underground are heaved up to the surface with the passing seasons. If I had to see that at actual water-boiling speed, it would be terrifying. As it happens so slowly, though, it just makes me ruminate on the nature of change, which is kind of comfortable. The flowers bloom and die, but their return is so much to be trusted that their death isn't sad. You just wait a while and they come back. Maybe they change their colors a bit, maybe they slide downhill a foot or so, but they come back. A garden gives you things to look forward to, seeing where the daffodils are going to travel, which variety of tomatoes will taste best, which will last through Thanksgiving, or whether the iron nails you sunk into the soil under the hydrangea will change the color of the blooms. You are given time and chances to figure out problems.

There was a drum composter in the back yard of that house that turned with a handle. I could put things in but there wasn't an easy way to get compost out. It took on a lot of water when it rained, and the water would slosh around when I cranked the handle. I figured out I could dump that water in which the compost had steeped. It made a "compost tea" that made the plants sing the halleluiah chorus.

My favorite plant in that back yard was the purple smoke tree. Bronze leaves framed delicate poufs of magenta that would turn mist-colored as they aged. After a rain it looked like the tree was holding clouds of smoke. More even than the creamy calla lilies, more than the deep blue stems of the false indigo, the smoke bush ministered to me with its beauty. Every evening when I would visit the yard it looked different. I would put my hand on its limbs, sometimes whispering "thank you." When a yard man clearing ice damaged trees cut it down, (I made the mistake of putting my hand on it and saying, "Don't touch this tree. I love this tree like I love my children") my heart broke in two. When a being gives you a sip of pure joy every day, how in the world could you not love it with your very bones? Even with the pain of loss and change, how could you not want to live choosing, in Martin Buber's words, an "I-Thou" relationship rather than "I-It" with as many beings as possible? That tree had been my friend.

A garden is not something you have to be good at. It will take whatever you can give. It has a life of its own, and it can be happy without you. It's happiest with you, though, as you putter through it in the afternoons after work, snipping off the things that are stealing the plant's energy, putting some mulch over roots when that will make them more comfortable, stroking the flowers, taking some into the house, watching the butterflies. You make a garden, in some ways, but the earth made it first, the seeds, the sprouts, the fruits. You're working with the earth, the sun and the shade, the sky and the wind to live in and amongst their beauty, tuned in to their rhythms, pulling blankets around the tender plants when a frost comes, moving things around until they are growing well. And sometimes having your heart broken when a beloved tree dies when it shouldn't have had to. Planting, sprouting, budding, blossoming, fruiting, seeding, dying; all the cycles are everywhere.

My Family's Religion

$\mathcal{3}\!\!\!\!\sim\!\!\!\! 9$

In the Christian seminary where I studied for three years, we were reminded that God is the Alpha and the Omega, which are the letters which begin and end the Greek alphabet. Our God was a God of history, they said, of this thing happening, then that thing, this causing that, a punishment or a reward for deeds, certain peoples destined for greatness, others for subjugation. Events happen in a line. The best thoughts were linear, arguments should move from point to point, traveling in straight lines. Cycles were for pagans, for people who aligned themselves with the seasons of the earth, the phases of the moon, and the longest and shortest days of the year. Pagans were interested in crops and rain, in sex and children. We People of the Book, readers of the Bible, Jews, Christians and Muslims, Baha'i, were people of history. We didn't care about cycles. We Christians were interested in salvation, which to my people meant correctness of belief, pleasing God by doing His will, surrendering to the Bible's teaching, living lives of righteousness. These were "higher things" than food, water, sex, or children, higher paths to joy.

I tried hard to be a Christian. I prayed, I did what I thought of as God's will, I was a good person. My spirit was naturally pagan. I noticed the moon and its phases. I nodded to it in reverence when it was full shining. I learned that when I could easily make its shape with my right hand, it was returning, and when I could make its shape with my left it was leaving. Placing offerings of flowers at the bases of big trees was something I was drawn to do. When my father's older sister Ruth visited, she spoke to me about the world of witches. That's what we were, generations back, she said. She'd been trained in England, she said. I can't remember the level she told me she'd reached. I remember the levels had different colors, like the karate belts I earned later on, but I don't remember what color she said she was. From her, when I was fifteen, I learned to read palms and Tarot cards. The Major Arcana, The Priestess, The Moon, The Hierophant and the Fool were the archetypes, she said. She'd trained as a Jungian analyst. Not in Zurich, I think, as the official training demanded in those days, but in some other sidewise way. She said she used to go to the coffee shops in Cambridge where she worked as a psychiatrist, and she would give free readings in hopes of being able to give some good advice to the young people there, some direction for their lives. "You know, I never once had to fake a reading. The cards always knew what the person sitting across from me needed to hear." Soaking her in, receptive to all of her stories, I listened, wide-eyed. A few years ago, when I visited her younger sister Dorothy in San Francisco, we were telling family stories. Asking about some that Aunt Ruth had told me, Dorothy snorted "Oh, Ruth was such a liar."

As I said, Aunt Ruth taught me palm reading. Tracing her fingers over my life line, my heart line, my life line, she talked about what the shape of fingers meant, about the thickness of the pad beneath the thumb, the lines across the wrist.

She told me we were descended from witches, that Giles Corey, squashed under rocks in Massachusetts, was an ancestor. I don't think he was any kind of a witch, and I hear Dorothy's words whenever I remember an Aunt Ruth story. It's too bad, really. My life had a little more color when I believed everything Ruth had said.

At Princeton Seminary in the late 70s the women were reading about the feminine face of God, reading Mary Daly, and realizing that once you started to call God "she," everything changed. The Biblical God had all of their femaleness erased as writers and historians revised and edited the manuscripts. The change worked on me gradually, gently rubbing away the accretions of orthodoxy, lightening the load of ideas I'd thought I couldn't live without.

When my then-husband and I moved to the Carolinas, I settled in to my job as Chaplain at the Women's College in town. Mark got his PhD at Duke, traveling up there once a week, staying for a few days, then coming home. Eventually he was settled as the minister of an old church in the western part of town, a church founded in 1765. As my Christianity got so thin and worn out that I could see through it, I began to move away from attending all the worship services. I wandered down the hill into the woods by the church. At the bottom of a hill was a spring. Clearing rotted leaves and weeds away, I freed up its flow, and I could sit and listen to the sound it made for long stolen moments.

There were two women my age at the church who were a bit witchy. I showed them the spring. After a time we formed a women's spirituality group that became a tight, joyous, and fractious sisterhood. We had Circle on Sabbats and full moons, season after season, in a glade protected by trees, broad fields and creek-water. Our altars were made of stones and tree stumps. We had knives and fire, drums and stars. It was as if, every step of the way, our spirits were remembering things we'd once known. We experimented with rhythms, we read *Where the Spirits Ride the Wind* and tried trances. We honored the ancestors and fed the spirits with bread and whiskey. We didn't know what we were doing. Reading books and experimenting, talking and dreaming, we took what was handed down and made the rest up ourselves, forming religion the way it has been formed always, by people just feeling their way. The cyclical nature of that religion felt right. We made prayers for birth, for children, for food, for the planet, for our work problems, relationship problems, and for our spirit problems. It was ecstatic and sensible and fun. Even though witchy Aunt Ruth was an Episcopal priest and swore that witchiness and Christly-ness went together just fine, my Christianity leaked out little by little. It was as if I'd been wearing an uncomfortable sweater with one loose thread. I had pulled on it by starting to call God "she" and it all unraveled. When I found myself with a pile of yarn at my feet, I started to make something else out of it.

My opinion now is that since all religions are made up by people, in one way or another, I will choose the one that makes sense for me and my life. I've often thought that, if I were to make up a religion for myself and those I love, it would have as its central metaphor the life cycle of a seed. I'm no botanist, I'm a theologian, a songwriter and a story teller, so I've used my sketchy understanding of the life cycle of a seed as a way of thinking about my life. I hope you will forgive my lack of scientific precision send me some grace, and find something here that nourishes your roots and your greening.

Rebellion in My Heart

Opening scene: Summer in North Carolina, the Fourth of July family reunion is in full swing. There is a long picnic table covered in a red and white checked oilcloth. On the table are set fried chicken, corn on the cob, watermelon, salad, green beans and potato chips. Sixty or so elders, middle aged folks, young parents and children mingle and perspire genteelly outside in the heat at Hopewell Farm. The adults talk in small groups and the children scream (not genteelly) and shoot each other with water guns. Once in a while an adult gets caught in crossfire. Stern words are half-heartedly spoken, followed by a brief period of quiet before the squealing water fight begins again. The stern words are mostly for show, and it is widely known which adults have supplied the children with the super-soakers.

I'm the family's published writer, and they are proud of me. Asked what writing projects I was working on currently, I perhaps unwisely answered, "I've been thinking about writing about my own life, you know, this family, my dad's family, the things I've learned over the years," I answer.

Ten minutes later my Uncle Harold, using my full childhood name, "Margaret Annie," asks for a word behind the house. I follow him out of sight of the others. He points his finger at me and starts talking about how he knows all about me and my life, how he knows all about Unitarian Universalism, the faith in which I'm a minister now, a far cry from the conservative Scottish Associate Reformed Presbyterian church in which I was reared. He knows all about everything, he says, red faced, angry, actually shaking his finger in my face, and he says I better not write anything embarrassing about this family. I'm a black belt in karate by then, and if anyone else shook a finger in my face this way I would take hold of it and try to resist the temptation to break it. Uncle Harold is eighty, and I was taught to respect my elders. I stood there, horrified and embarrassed, until I remembered Anne Lamott writing, "You own everything that happened to you. Tell your stories. If people wanted you to write warmly about them, they should have behaved better." While he was still scolding I made the decision to start a memoir with this scene.

The family is an upstanding and fine group of people saturated in righteousness and moved by the effort to be the people God calls them to be. I had no idea what embarrassing things he might be talking about. My mother grew up in India, the child of missionaries. She, her sister and two brothers played with cow patties in the dust with the children of whatever village they were missionary-ing in at the time. At a British boarding school in the Himalaya Mountains, she ran track at 7,000 feet and learned rude songs about the King of England. In the dining hall you'd ask for the bread rolls to be passed, and the kid who had the bread would say "Air Mail or Freight"? Air Mail meant they threw you the roll, and Freight meant they'd squash it, pass it to the next kid, who would squash it, and so on until it got to you. When Partition happened in 1947, creating the two independent countries of India and Pakistan, missionaries were forced to go home. Mama, her sister and two brothers (Harold was the younger brother) came back to the States longing for India, having no idea of the customs, music, styles or culture of the kids they were put in school with. They'd always dressed from the "missionary barrel," where church people put their old worn out clothes. It felt like finery until they saw the faces of relatives who met them at the docks when they came home for furlough. The welcoming faces fell, and the relatives looked away, embarrassed. She would tell me this story when I fussed about a stain on a shirt or a safety pin holding up a hem. "Just throw your shoulders back and smile, Meggie, and no one will notice!" she trilled.

As soon as she got to college, Mama joined the International Students group, and relaxed among people with as little idea as she had about the America in which she found herself.

At home, when my sister and I were children, she made curry and chapatis, milky tea and "Roti mak en chini," which means bread with butter and sugar on it. We heard her singing in Urdu as she washed dishes, and never learned any other word for the person who fixes shoes than "muochi," which I'm not sure I'm spelling correctly. When her brothers and sisters would get together, they'd cook a big pot of curry, with the oldest sister standing guard so Harold wouldn't sneak in and add a few more shakes of heat to the pot. They would giggle as they told us about the times when they were on furlough in the States, traveling around the South giving presentations on their mission work. "Say something in Urdu!" one of the parents would command, and they'd say shocking things their teetotaler parents wouldn't understand, like "Please pass the beer." And "I'll have a whisky!"

Mama never did get the hang of the US completely. She swore that you had to pay the postman or he wouldn't deliver your mail, which is how it had been in India. One time she phoned the police station and asked how late they were open. "Lady, this is the police. We're always open." She got to know the local police due to her lead foot, always insisting on a "vroom vroom car," meaning that it had a standard transmission. "Wheeeee!" was a sound she often made when she was behind the wheel.

When I was born, my parents were both students at Princeton Theological Seminary. Mama was in the Christian Educator program, and my father was studying for the Presbyterian ministry. He had wanted to be an opera singer, but his father, a renowned evangelist with an enormous personality, would not hear of that. Instead of being a singer, he went into doctoral studies in nuclear physics. Then the bomb was dropped, and job offers poured in. He went on some interviews, but didn't like the idea of the white coated scientists as future co-workers. He quit grad school and taught math at a school near Princeton. Even the math teacher had to teach religion too, in those days, and he couldn't do that without his deeply held Christianity coming through. Threatened with dismissal, he decided to get seminary training so he could teach religion the way he wanted to. He met and married Mama, the young woman from India by way of North Carolina, and I was born before they graduated. When I got to Princeton Seminary, I was twenty-two, and many of the professors who remembered my parents had their mid-life crises triggered as they gasped "You're Baby Margaret"?

The first job my dad got after they graduated was as Billy Graham's reader. "I preach," he told my father. "You read the books and underline the parts I can preach from." We moved to Black Mountain, NC, where the Grahams had their home. I remember Mama walking with toddler-me around the shady paths of Montreat, the Presbyterian retreat center where we lived. We'd stop on the stone bridges and lean over to look at the cool creeks, dropping leaves into the water to see how fast they sailed away. We'd find little chunks of mica and peel the layers, watching the translucent flakes sparkle in the sunshine.

I was girly enough to want full skirts and petticoats, which my mother would sew. My little sister was born, and Mama sewed her the same things she'd made for me so we matched. I also wanted a holster and a pair of cowgirl six-guns too, but I was somehow unable to make that happen.

More than anything, more than wanting to be a ballerina, more than I wanted petticoats and six-guns, through my whole girlhood, I wanted a horse. Every birthday or Christmas my parents would tell me they couldn't afford a horse, and where would we keep it? I chose to believe that they were just trying to throw me off the scent with misdirection, and that, on the day, I'd get a beautiful horse. When I didn't get one, year after year, in my innate optimism I was certain it would happen the next year.

My mother was sad there at Montreat. Stories differ, but she felt my dad was spending too much time and emotional energy on a tall Nordic blonde in their Bible study group who was unhappily married. When the blonde lady left for Florida my dad went after her. To leave his marriage? To go retrieve her for her husband? As I say, stories differ, but Mama took my sister and me away from Black Mountain and moved in with my evangelist grandfather at his "farm" in Doylestown, PA. We'd lived there before when Graham was having an extended NY "Crusade," and my dad would come see us on his days off. I remember love from back then. One of my earliest memories is of him coming in the door in an overcoat, a London Fog kind of coat with a faux fur collar. He was tall and smiling, wearing glasses. He came in the door shouting hello. Mama and I were hiding behind the door and we jumped out, to be enveloped in an enormous bear hug, big enough for both of us.

Another memory from that early time at the farm is of a field of daffodils in front of the house, stretching as far as I could see. The huge yellow flowers were at eye level. I filled my arms with picked flowers, transported by their scent. When my mother went to take them from me so we could carry them back up to the house, I insisted that I could do it. Whether I succeeded is not part of the memory, but, given the way that I am still scalded by any failure, I think I'd have remembered if I'd dropped my fragrant jubilation.

Back at the farmhouse, my sad mother was taken under the wing of the Big Man's new wife, my dad's step-mother, and fault lines were drawn.

In the summer the split rail fence that marked the beginning of the daffodil pasture was covered with yellow climbing roses. At the bottom of the daffodil pasture was a small pond where my sister and I learned to ice skate in the winter.

When kindergarten started in the fall, I rode a palomino pony named Topsy through a field of grain to the school bus stop. Mama would walk with us and show me how to pick the kernels of grain and pop them in my mouth. If she wasn't with us, when we reached the bus stop I would just hug Topsy, smack him gently on the rump, and he'd trundle on back to the farm. It was a working farm, sort of. My grandfather bought it thinking he could feed the family and maybe some German refugees in case of the end of the world, or some equivalent disaster. There were chickens, crops of some kind, a swimming pool, a barn, and a big stone farm house.

The job with Graham was over, and, since it looked like his family was holed up at the farm more or less permanently, my father moved back to Philadelphia, close enough to Doylestown to visit often. Grandfather's new wife was in residence, though. To my father, she was the wicked step-monster, so Mama was in a righteous fortress. The gates opened to admit the wayward husband so he could be a dad. I guess it worked pretty well for all concerned, except for my dad. I don't know. I was five.

I got teased on the bus. I was a fat kid, and my eyes were crossed. The optic nerve in the right eye never connected properly, even after surgeries to straighten out my eyes. The eye doctor had put a patch over my good eye that year, in hopes that the other optic nerve would attach and start working. I held my head up and tried to think of myself as a pirate. I tried to adopt a devil-may-care attitude about the eye patch and the bullying.

The class had two teachers, Miss Margaret and Miss Lillian. Miss Margaret played the flute and Miss Lillian played the harp. I remember two incidents from that year. One was that my friend with red and white striped cat-eye glasses told me she couldn't be my friend anymore because she was now going to be friends with that girl over there. Bewildered, I tried to absorb the rule I hadn't known, that you could only be friends with one person at a time. The other thing I remember was the embarrassing incident where I scooted closer and closer to a boy I liked as we sat on the stage in some kind of performance. Maybe he was my new friend to take the place of candy striped cat-eye glasses girl. Miss Margaret or Miss Lillian felt she had to come up on the stage, pick me up under my arms and deposit me back in my original place. I remember the light reflecting off my father's glasses in the audience. I don't remember what I liked about that boy. I remember the chagrin of being moved away from him, though. Teachers had a lot of rules I didn't know. I didn't like finding out about them by breaking them.

I still remember the feeling of that time spent with Mama riding slowly through the sun-dappled grain field. She was a believer in time spent together. We went on six-week camping trips every summer, all over the US, Scandinavia, Britain and Europe. We had dinner every night together as a family, we watched Sonny and Cher and Carol Burnett and laughed our heads off. We watched Star Trek, groaning as the crew member in the red shirt went between boulders on some godforsaken planet and was never seen again. We teased Mom about her after-work nap and about her singing songs in Urdu as she washed the dishes. I carry her in my heart, though she died of breast cancer when I was twenty-three. I can still hear the dish-washing song, though when I try to recreate it for an actual speaker of Urdu they shake their heads, mystified by the syllables I've misremembered. I love red geraniums, as she did, long car trips, and drumming. She carried a love of the drums from her childhood in India, and would turn up the drum solos in the rock songs on the car radio.

The Big Man died when I was in the middle of first grade, and we left Topsy in Doylestown and my dad in Philadelphia and moved to North Carolina to live with her parents. Suddenly surrounded by the southern cousins, we settled into Mama's world with our father in the far distance.

I started second grade in Miss Speaks' class at the Mulberry Street Elementary School. . She was young and fun and kind, and my favorite thing she would say, in her Carolina drawl, was "Let's take out a new piece of paper and start fresh. " Staaaart frayush, was the way she almost sang it, her voice rising high on the first word and swooping down, resolving on the second. Here came a sense of possibility, of handwriting and math messes which could be avoided this time. The fresh paper was ignorant of my character, my inability to follow instructions, my handwriting which would start carefully perfect and deteriorate fast as the writing took on momentum. The fresh sheet had no prejudgments. It wasn't braced for the teacher to sigh as she inspected my work.

In third grade the teacher was elderly, mean and burned out. If you tapped her shoulder to ask her something, she'd snap "Do I have a bug on me or something"? She weighed the class and posted our weights on the wall. Why would a teacher do that? I was second from the top of the girls and the boys.

In the third grade play I got to sing a patriotic number about George Washington. "First in war, first in peace, first in the hearts of his countrymen." I remember flags and maybe a fife and drum. It was fun to sing in front of people. In the cafeteria I remember turnip greens, cornbread and fatback for lunch. Mama taught fifth grade at that same school, and she had some teenaged boys who had flunked a grade two or three times. She was mad at their parents, who, she said, ruined their brains by feeding them a breakfast of "An RC Cola and a MoonPie." She was a health food nut early on in the movement, reading Adele Davis and Rachel Carson. We ate honey instead of sugar, whole grains, and real butter instead of margarine. One time she brought home kelp cookies, but that wasn't until the early 70s. When we were toddlers, she would reward good behavior with celery. "Hooray, celery!" we would crow. When I found out about candy I knew I'd been betrayed.

Miss Foster, my fourth grade teacher, was tall and elegant, and she wore her hair in a French Twist. One morning halfway through the year, the "scout" kids who would watch the hall from the classroom doorway hissed "She's coming! She's got a new hair-do!" That was headline news to us. Soon after that she got married, but I can't remember what her new name was. My best friend's name was Pam. She had red hair and freckles, and I thought she did the best imitation of an English accent ever when we sang Beatles' songs together. We'd sit, or really, in those days without seat belts, we'd roll around in the backs of our mom's station wagons in the "way back," singing at the top of our lungs around the curves which threw us to one side and then another. "I wanna hold your haaaaand!" At recess we played horse, galloping around the playground, or we played "George Washington's spies," galloping or stepping lightly as we could when we were being sneaky. We tried to learn to walk on fallen leaves without making a sound. She and I would go horseback riding at her house in the country and be spies some more, galloping fast as the wind..

The cousins and I would ride horses at Uncle David's house. His back yard was several acres of pastureland, and there were three or four horses. We rode a palomino Quarter Horse, a shaggy brown pony named Molly, and a dappled gray Tennessee Walking Horse named New Look. My cousin Rebecca and I would ride down to the Bottomland, a clearing with rich dark soil where water would collect after a storm. There would be fallen logs and little rocks to jump over, if you could get the horse to jump. It felt good being surrounded by family. You knew who you were from the family stories, from the inside jokes, from the way you were taught not to whine or cuss or have a bad day, from the way we took care of each other, from the way you got ignored if you were sick as if it were rude, from all of the men being either doctors or ministers, from all the women being stay at home moms or teachers, and from the way no one laughed at the way you talked.

In the summers, Mom took both of us with her to Appalachian State or UNC Chapel Hill so she could get her Master's Degree. I think there was a woman who knitted who was in charge of watching us, but mostly I remember walking by ourselves to the pool, working up the courage to go off of the highest diving board, meeting Mama at the Circus Room for lunch. The Circus Room was the first time we'd felt air conditioning. It was delicious and exotic. I made a friend that summer and all we did was play pirates. We had swordfights and pretended to tie people up. The knitter taught me to knit. When Mama had to go to class during the school year once in a while, our older cousin Ed would watch us. He let us do pretty much anything we wanted. It was under his supervision that I learned how awful it was to have orange juice with bologna, and that orange juice after toothpaste is terrible.

Lilith

ॐ

Before we moved in with Grandmother and
Grandfather, we spent a few months with Aunt
Jean, whose house was right across a small brown
pond from my grandparents' house. Next to Aunt
Jean's was an exotic neighbor family, the
Grunwalds. The dad was a designer for a North
Carolina furniture factory. I think he was German.
Mrs. Grunwald was a tall, slender woman who wore
her hair up in a French chignon. It could be that my
missionary family, with our oriental rugs, Indian
brass and carved teak, were exotic to them too. In
the Grunwalds' house were glass walls and polished
blonde wood floors, sleek European furniture on
geometric-patterned rugs. I remember oranges and
yellows and a cheery quiet. Their daughter was
named Lilith. Years later I learned that in ancient
tradition, Lilith was Adam's first wife, before Eve.
She was so wild and disobedient that she was
banned from Eden and replaced with the nicer,
sweeter woman, Eve. That they would name their
daughter after this wild force of nature tells me I'm
not wrong in remembering them as a contrast to my
church-going, Bible reading family.

Mrs. Grunwald was elegant. When my nose
itched up inside, I would poke a finger in and
scratch. Mama told me to brush the outside of my
nose lightly when it itched inside, that was how Mrs.

Grunwald did it, and wasn't she lovely? Mama wanted to be tall and elegant instead of cute and perky, and Mrs. Grunwald was her ideal.

Lilith and I used to go down to the pond in the back yard to fish. We each had a stick with string tied to the end with a safety pin onto which we might hook a worm. Most of the time we didn't put on any worms. We knew nothing about flies or lures. We never did catch anything, but I looked into the brown water and felt happy fishing with my friend, talking about nothing much.

The world of my grandparents revolved around the church, the Bible, the Lord. Few sentences were spoken without reference to one of these. Lilith's family talked about food, politics, travel, their time living in India, where Lilith was born.

Neither of us was as wild and disobedient as Lilith's namesake. I was a good little girl. I tried hard to be, anyway. I know I thought about God a lot, and I worried that He was disappointed in me. I knew my teachers always were, because I couldn't follow instructions. To them it looked like rebellion, but really it was an inability to fathom why the rules were there. Why does it matter that I write my name on the upper right hand corner of the paper? Why can't I get out of my seat to see what that noise is in the hall? I broke them because I couldn't keep them in mind.

Eventually I was expelled from that Eden, from the heartfelt and dedicated certainties of my family's religion. Really, I just walked out of the garden. I couldn't keep the theological rules in mind. They didn't make sense to me, and I took it all so seriously that I needed a theology that made sense. I didn't know that many of the others were just letting the doctrines lay in layers as a restful backdrop to real life, and there I was trying to grab all the pieces and fit them together. I couldn't make it happen and I couldn't let it go, so I threw up my hands and left.

I didn't become disobedient and disruptive. Until recently. Now I'm a Lilith for sure. I run back and forth outside the wall of the garden of certainties, jumping up to see the remembered landscape, pointing and questioning. "Do you know this thing is there? Does that one not bother you? If I can get this gate open, don't some of y'all want to come out here with me"? Most people in the garden of certainty don't want to come out with me. Certainty is hard to let go of. It was hard for me to let it go, but I couldn't stay. I remain fascinated by friends who didn't grow up in the church at all, people who have a vague notion of who Abraham is, but who couldn't tell you who his children and grandchildren were. What did their family talk about? What did they push against? What gave them comfort? Where did their sense of the world come from, their sense of what had been and was yet to be? I'm grateful to Lilith and her family for a brief and elegant glimpse of another way to be, a glimpse of a different way to be in the world, outside the walls I'd assumed surrounded everyone.

Rebellion in My Heart 2

ॐ

Negotiations had been going on, unbeknownst to my sister and me, for a reconciliation between our mother and father. Powerful forces leaned on my mother, and she packed us up and moved us back north. Before we left, all the cousins gathered in the back bedroom of Uncle David and Aunt Anita's house, focusing their attention on me. "Margaret Ann," they intoned, "You must swear. You SWEAR that even if you are moving to The North you will always remain a Rebel in your heart." To me, the word "rebel" meant canny, independent, and ready to question authority. I nodded solemnly. "Say it!" they said "May my eyes turn to applesauce and my guts turn to barbed wire if I do not always remain a rebel in my heart." I said it. I think, according to my definition, I've done pretty well by that oath.

We moved the summer I turned ten, and spent it in a rented house at the Jersey shore. The reconciliation was doomed from the start. Our family's house was a couple of blocks from my father's secretary Carol's house. We socialized with her family all summer. Carol was slender and blonde, perky yet sophisticated. She would say in a fake self-deprecating voice "Some people say I look like a Breck girl," talking about the perfect blonde beauties on the back of most women's magazines back in that day. I'd been fortunate up until then not to have any adults in my life who liked to humiliate children. Carol enjoyed it. She made terrible fun of our southern accents. She'd call people over and say "Listen to this! Say 'Sprite,' and then they'd all laugh. One time we were all having sandwiches and I said I didn't want mayonnaise, thank you. She announced to the group that I didn't like mayonnaise, and had they ever heard such a thing?

I hated her, and it didn't help when Mama soon realized that my dad was in love with her, and had been, somehow, since he was seventeen. I don't know how far their relationship went. Her two children were named the same names as my dad's sister and brother, and her daughter had the same hereditary eye problem I got from my dad. He swears they're not his children. Yes, years, later, I asked him. Did he lie? I'll never know.

Mama got independent, and we went sailing every day. She had learned sailing as a counselor at camp. Lying on her application, she claimed to be a sailing teacher. "I just stayed a chapter ahead of the kids and it turned out just fine," she said cheerily. I didn't understand what all was going on with the grown-ups. My mother muttered darkly about "your father's harem," and once said, "He treats you more like a wife than me." I was ten. And that was true. Not sexually, but emotionally. My dad, who had lived Over There for years, now wanted to spend every moment with me, talking, playing chess, nagging me about eating fresh fruits and vegetables, getting exercise, doing math. Apparently, in the division that sometimes happens in families, I was to be my dad's and my younger sister was my mom's. They cooked together and talked about dieting. He talked to me as if I were an adult, his therapist, his friend. I felt chosen, grown up, but completely inadequate to the job. "I thought about going to a therapist one time," he confided, but a friend of the family said I would just run circles around any of them intellectually, so what would be the point?

Later on, when I worked as a therapist, I realized how dumb that was. Therapists don't try to do something to you that you then try to prevent them from doing. You work together, help each other. If you don't want to do it, don't do it, but don't pretend there is no one capable of cracking into your well-defended vault.

In the fall we bought a ranch house halfway up a hill in a western suburb of Philadelphia. My father lived in an apartment in the city. Mama was happy in that house, happy with the mimosa tree in the front yard, which reminded her of North Carolina, where they grow like weeds in the highway ditches. She was happy with her job teaching second grade at a school not too far away. My elementary school was just down at the bottom of our hill and we walked to and from school every day. I was lost in the fifth grade class, where the kids had already learned fractions, and I hadn't yet. My dad was a math teacher, though, so I caught up fast. He was working as a news analyst for the CBS news station in Philadelphia, and was on the news team on the six and eleven o'clock broadcasts. He'd come home in the afternoons, help with homework, have early dinner, drive back for the six o'clock broadcast, come back for the evening, chess, discussion, more homework, and then he'd go do the eleven o'clock broadcast and go home to his apartment in town. This felt normal to us. I don't know how my parents did it.

We played with the neighborhood kids, circling on our bikes late into the dusky darkness. Lisa went to Sacred Heart, Glen went to my school, and he was cool. The boys across the street had set their garage on fire on purpose, so they were off at a reform school and the house looked sad and closed up. My fifth grade teacher loved ceramics and square dancing, so we did plenty of both. I had a little trouble in square dancing because of a tendency to mix up my right and left hand. Finally Mrs. Greiner just wrote a big R on my right hand and an L on my left. I probably should have been humiliated, but it was actually kind of helpful. She took us to see an old dance caller in the Brandywine valley who also juggled medicine clubs that looked like big bowling pins. A man in a brown sports jacket pulled up in the driveway while we were there in the old man's yard listening to him tell stories. "This is my friend Andy Wyeth," he said to us. I knew who he was, and I knew his father's work too. Many of the books I'd been given for Christmas over the years had illustrations by NC Wyeth. *Knights and Ladies, Robin Hood, The Scarlett Pimpernel.*

Ballerina had been my first career choice, but ballet teachers weren't encouraging to a pudgy girl.

Still, I trained myself to fall asleep on my back, with one leg straight out and the other bent, with my toe pointed at the straight leg's knee; one arm was on the pillow above my head and the other curved in front of my body. That felt ballerina-ish to me. I didn't know why I didn't wake up in that position. My room was decorated with lilac wallpaper with ballerinas drawn on it everywhere.

I didn't know being a writer was a possibility. My second career choice was to take care of horses, to curry them, rake out the stalls, ride them, jump them, and smell them. The mid-century ranch bedrooms had long windows, set high into the wall. On the deep window sills, I set up my collection of Breyer plastic horses. Every evening I would "feed" them, which took some time, as there were maybe thirty of them. One of the first times I was aware of money was when I'd gotten six dollars, maybe for an allowance, maybe for babysitting my sister. I never paid much attention to money. Mama would tease me about using my allowance for a bookmark. I was walking fast toward the store to buy a new model horse, and I had the dollars fanned out in front of me. They looked beautiful, because I could turn them into a horse!

When I was ten, I wrote a story about a balloonist named Mme. Featherflight and a small boy who stowed away on her balloon when she had landed at the fair. By the time she found him, it was too late to take him home, so they saw the world together and had adventures. My dad was captivated by this story, and swore to me for the rest of my life that I was a writer. When my first book was published he was upset by what I wrote and how I saw things, so he never read any of the others. Until the end, he said I should write children's books. This made me mad. I wrote one by accident and one on purpose, but I never mentioned them to him. Bless both our hearts.

Still he gave me my comfort with thinking of myself as a writer. I don't know if fathers understand how much of a daughter's identity comes through him. I have always felt gorgeous, even though I know the truth of how I look, because he called me "gorgeous" every day. It was his greeting to me. I have looked at pictures of myself from those days, a bit pudgy, both buck toothed and cross-eyed, but I have felt gorgeous in my essence my whole life because of that.

The attention and emotion that came at me from the little Mme. Featherflight story spooked me, maybe, so I didn't write anything else for a long time.

My chosen work, as a child, was as a counselor. My mother and sister fought a lot, and I'd jump in the middle. I could see they were talking past one another, and if I could help them understand what the other one was saying maybe the fight would stop. Mostly they got mad at me and told me to butt out. My father talked to me about his life. Too much. He confided that he'd had suicidal thoughts when he was younger. That knowledge never left my mind. He wanted to play chess, I would play chess. He wanted me to sing while he played the piano, I would sing. He wanted to teach me the essentials of music theory, I would try to learn. To this day when someone tries to explain music theory to me I begin to burn inside. There is a roaring in my ears. I feel like someone is holding a pillow over my face, and I will shove as hard as I need to in order to breathe again.

In sixth grade we had two teachers, Mr. Murray and Mr. Princevali. Mr. Murray had wavy silver hair and glasses. He was kind and slow-talking, thorough. Mr. P was young, skinny, and dark-haired. His teaching was sparky and confident, almost self-righteous, but not in a bad way. He taught math and science, and Mr. Murray taught everything else. After lunch we would put our heads down on our desks and he would read to us. That year we went through the *Iliad* and the *Odyssey*. I remember being surprised that people's emotions and motivations back then were the same as the ones I'd noticed people having in the present day. Maybe humans were just human all the time, in all times. I stored that away for future reference. We learned "new math" that year with Mr. P, sets and subsets and base three and base nine. He took us to a Swarthmore to show off to the college students how much we knew. I wish I still knew everything now that I knew then.

That sixth grade year I also learned how to run like a girl. Debbie Klutz, who was more developed than any of the rest of us, took us to the top of the playground hill and demonstrated how to run down while keeping your elbows tight to your sides to stabilize your breasts, which she already had. Then you were supposed to fling your hands and forearms back and forth as you ran, creating a fetching picture of wiggly femininity. I watched, but was not convinced.

New Name

৺

I felt like a failure in the squealy wiggly model of girl hood. I wasn't sure what kind of girl I was, or what kind I wanted to be. I knew I was tired of the exasperated way people would say my name. "Ay-unn, you're so bright, why can't you follow instructions!" "Ay-unn, you need to have pride in the neatness of your papers. These are just messy."

I knew Meg was short for Margaret, so I announced in sixth grade that everyone was to call me Meg. The exasperation I expected when a teacher would say my name didn't happen much from then on. I'm not sure what else changed, but when a person changes what they want to be called, you may be sure other changes are crowding into the wings, waiting for their turn on the stage. Then Franco Zefferelli's *Romeo and Juliet* was released. Olivia Hussy played a young woman who was not at all wiggly, who was like a clear stream of a girl, a fair moon of a girl, so I parted my black hair in the middle like her black hair. I wanted to be Meg, a fair moon of a girl, a clear stream of a girl.

When we would visit the family in North Carolina, they all still called me Margaret Annie. It's hard to keep your new self together when you go back home where they knew you before. We'd stay again with Grandmother and Grandfather in the square two-story red brick house on Sullivan Road, surrounded by brass bowls and mahogany furniture from India. Grandmother had thick eyebrows and didn't wear a bra. She wore shirtwaist dresses and cooked with no salt. It's not that she was trying to cook in a healthy way, she just never learned to cook because when they lived in India, they always had a cook. Grandfather was a tall lean man, balding and funny. He would toast marshmallows for us over the burners of the electric stove, and he'd sing "I'd rather have fingers than toes. I'd rather have ears than a nose. But as for my hair, I'm glad that it's there, I sure will be sorry if it goes," and then he'd grin and pass his hand over his bald head. When we were in the car together, with my mom driving, Grandmother would grab the panic handle above the door, put her other hand over her heart and exclaim "Oh my conscience!" One of the memories that mystifies me is that one day I was home with a terrible earache. I never felt such pain. Grandmother and grandfather were on the first floor where they lived, and I was on the second floor where we lived. We were downstairs all the time, for meals, to watch TV, for prayers. I was moaning aloud because it hurt so badly, but no one came up to check on me. No one brought soup or aspirin or anything a normal family might do for someone who was sick. It was always as if, when you were sick, you were doing something shameful that should be ignored. She wasn't an unkind woman, but I don't know why that day happened the way it did. The next time I was sick with measles, Mama took me to Aunt Anita and Uncle David's house.

Grandmother talked about The Lord all the time, and sometimes would look at me, misty-eyed, and say "You have your whole life ahead of you." A smart woman who wanted to preach in those days would just go be a missionary. They were allowed to teach other women, and sometimes could help their husbands preach.

When amongst the southern family, we were not allowed to swear in any way. We were told that Uncle David had called his brother a fool once, in a heated childhood fight. Their father, my Great Grandfather, a devout ARP preacher, took him into a back room where they knelt together and prayed earnestly that God would spare him from the damnation promised in the Scripture to anyone who used that word about a brother. Taking the Lord's name in vain was also completely taboo. Of course we would never say "Oh, my God." Even Gosh, Golly, or the Carolinian kid's "Gah" were forbidden, as they were just a sneaky way to take God's name in vain. Other NC ARP rules had to do with behavior on the Sabbath. That's what we called Sunday. It would be easier to give you the list of what was allowed than what wasn't. Going to Sunday School was a given, going to church, having family meals, Bible study, Bible memorization games, naps, and going to "Vespers," an evening service at church, then prayers and bed time. That's all we could do. On one Easter visit, when a sunrise service had been added to the normal three-times-church a Sunday, I locked myself in the bathroom at my Aunt Edith's house and refused to go to Vespers. "No more church!" I said. "That's enough!" I remember my mom and her big sister, the enforcer, Aunt Edith, talking to me through the door, but I was an immovable object. At least that's how I remember it. There was no swimming on Sabbath, no music other than church music. No dancing, no playing cards, no board games. I remember one cousin setting the alarm for midnight, just to get up, put on a 45, and dance for a minute once it was technically not Sabbath any more. A goodly proportion of those cousins became lawyers, having had rules and legalism galore in which to find loopholes beginning in childhood.

Mama would bend rules for us. On Sabbath we'd play Battleships, but she'd call it "Going to Jerusalem," and the filled-in squares would be our donkeys laden with goods that we were taking up the dangerous road to Jerusalem. Bandits would shoot at us, calling out "F-7!"

"Oh, man, you shot my donkey."

The rules after we moved north to be with my dad were much different. The Enforcer was all the way down in North Carolina. At first we went to a gigantic gray stone Presbyterian church in Bryn Mawr where the kids got sex education and the preaching was about kindness and justice. In the church art gallery at one point there was an exhibit of sculptures by Brancusi. The minister was a tall dignified man who, one Sunday, quoted a song with a sonorous voice to make a point in his sermon "If you are going to San Francisco, be sure to wear some flowers in your hair." I don't remember anything else he ever preached about. I just remember being half impressed and half horrified that he had taken something from my world and somehow dragged it into his world. I don't know why we changed churches. The reasons people do that are myriad, and sometimes unknown even to them. Our next church was a small Presbyterian church in Valley Forge where the minister was running off anti-Vietnam war pamphlets in the basement on the church mimeograph machine.

My father, who read the Bible deeply, daily, was a fighter for civil rights, for affirmative action, for government aid to struggling foreign countries and to the poor of our own country. He was not anti-war, though, and he thought our minister was a Communist. I don't know where my dad went to church. He believed in Nixon to the end, telling me that the President knew many things we did not know, and he surely had good reasons for the Watergate break-in. I thought Nixon was a crook. He told me not to be a dupe of the Communists. We talked politics and theology at the dinner table. He worked as a news analyst and commentator for CBS, and we got the benefit of all of his research.

We heard about the origins of the tensions in African and Middle-Eastern countries, about the Hutu and the Tutsi, the Palestinians and the Jews, the Koreans and the Japanese. The bad part was being called on at dinner to give an impromptu explanation for something in the news.

With the move north, the family culture around being sick or injured stayed the same. I remember one time telling Mama I had a headache. "Oh

Honey," she said brightly, "Children don't get headaches!" My dad would come home every afternoon, open the front door and call out, "Everybody happy?!" Not being happy was not an option we were offered. If I was having a bad day, I knew I should just keep it to myself.

Speaking to the Locks

⁓

I had a significant dream when I was thirteen, a dream that shaped my life. In the dream a gray-haired woman in a white coat sat behind a desk. I knew she was me, far in the future. Behind her on the wall was a cross-stitched sampler with a motto. I wish I could remember what it said. The words were the most beautiful words I had ever heard or read. I was moved to tears, lifted by the beauty of the message. As the dream went on, I saw a photograph of the same woman in a newspaper clipping. The caption below her picture is all I remember. In bold type, it read, "Speaking to the Locks." I woke up knowing what I was supposed to do with my life. I was going to "speak to the locks." I tucked that away, keeping the phrase like a smooth stone in my pocket, running my fingers over it, feeling its shape and solidity.

My father asked if I'd like to go to a private girl's school for seventh grade. The image of students in uniforms appealed to me. It seemed clean and simple, relaxing. Clothes had started to be such a signal in sixth grade. Debbie Klutz, the one who taught us how to run like girls, had tight cashmere sweaters and pencil skirts. I had no idea about what I wanted to look like, except maybe a combination of Robin Hood from the Errol Flynn movies and Maid Marian. Leggings of leather, a flowy something, and a bow and arrows. None of that was available in the stores at the mall, so it felt like it might be relaxing never to have to think about what to wear.

We shopped for uniforms twice. The first time one of my parents put the boxes on top of the car and drove off, so I'm not sure where those knee socks, gym tunics, pleated skirts, blazers and white shirts with Peter Pan collars went. I'm sure the saddle oxfords made some big-footed child a sturdy pair of shoes. The school was across the street from Bryn Mawr College. A black wrought-iron fence surrounded our campus. A fabulous Victorian house with a rounded front was where the boarding students lived. A covered stone walkway led to the low stone building where the classrooms and labs were. Weeping cherry trees lined the drive, along with enormous bronze-leafed copper beeches. The classes were first rate. At gym, I met my seventh-grade best friend, Ellen, whose brother later taught me to kiss. The next year brought an additional best friend, Carolyn. She was from West Philadelphia, warm and kind, with an amazing velvet voice and milk-chocolate skin. She was as tall as I was, and we stuck together instantly. I thought she looked like a queen, and I wanted to be just like her. There were lots of rich girls there, one of whom, I think, had her Bat Mitzvah on a safari in Kenya with all her friends. I'm not sure. I wasn't invited to that one.

My mother wasn't sure the school was a good thing. We were encouraged to ask questions in class, to discuss the Bible as literature, then the next semester, The Devil in Literature. She was concerned that I would turn into some kind of bluestocking. I had to look up what that was. She was especially horrified by the British woman who taught American History. "Those poor boys were seventeen years old, during the Boston Massacre," the teacher said. "The townspeople were throwing snowballs at them with rocks inside. That's why they opened fire." My Revolutionary War-loving mother called the headmistress in an outrage. Every time I said that teacher's name, Mama would sputter.

My dad had a new split level house built down the road. I don't know what their financial arrangements were. It seems strange to me now that my father made so many decisions about a house he would only sleep in on Christmas Eves. Christmas was major in our house, celebrated in German style, with the tree going up on Christmas Eve, decorated before the children went to bed. Presents would be piled under the tree. If a present had three parts, all three would be wrapped separately to make the pile higher. Then bedsheets would be hung over the doorways so everything was hidden. My father would be sleeping in the guest room, a very special occurrence indeed. We were to wake him with music. My sister would play the flute and I would play the guitar. We'd sing carols and he'd shamble out in his PJs, merry, merry, then get dressed and come down to breakfast. Breakfast was huge, and must be finished before the sheets were taken down and presents could be opened. He never drank coffee, but on Christmas morning he did. Then, when all the food was gone, he would say to my mother, "Kathy, I'd like another cup of coffee, please!" We would squeal in delighted torment. Finally the opening would begin. It took hours, because he would hand out a present and everyone would watch while you opened it. Until I was a teenager, Christmas was lovely. I was so surly as a teenager. Nothing seemed appealing but sex, drugs, and rock n roll. Really, it was just rock that was lovely. I'd fall asleep to Led Zeppelin every night, which bothered my dad greatly. "This is the time of night where you should be praying to God," he'd say. But Robert Plant's voice was so beguiling. Sex was ok, done because my boyfriend at the time was obsessed and insistent. It was just easier to do it than to listen to him whine. Drugs were available with my next boyfriend, who was the neighborhood prep school dealer. They were ok, but I usually preferred the company of my own playful and entertaining brain without chemical enhancement.

For my room in the new house, I asked the painters to pick out a green for the walls the color of new leaves in spring. Bless their hearts, they did not roll their eyes at the fourteen-year-old with her dark hair in her face. They did pretty well, choosing a soft gray-green. The Breyer horses went into boxes, I think. I'm not sure what happened to them. A green, red and white hand-stitched Amish quilt covered my bed. A dark green shag rug covered the floor. I loved doing my yoga on that rug. I had Richard Hittleman's sixty-day yoga book. The model was a white woman with blond hair, a white leotard and white lipstick. She sure could do those yoga poses. I worked my way through that book and got so flexible I could put my feet behind my head. I could stand on my head, I could do that exercise where you pull your stomach muscles in and snap them out. My dad didn't like me doing yoga. He told me if I spent as much time studying the Bible as I did doing yoga it would do me a lot more good. The main thing he didn't like, I think, was that it gave me a reason to be in my room when I was supposed to be available to him every minute when he was home. He visited every evening, and I understand now that he wanted to see me when he was there. My sister, who belonged more to my mother, was allowed to go to her room when he was there, but not I.

The demand for availability was oppressive. I was his best friend, I think. I was smart enough to talk to him, listen to him, play chess with him. I was teachable. I know now that he was lonely. Still, it's not fair to lock your daughter into being your daughter your companion and partner in life. That is emotional incest, which is pretty much what it was. It's not fun winning the contest between a daughter and a mother for which one the dad would rather hang out with. Psychologists talk about "the chosen child," and how you feel almost superhuman because one of your adults has picked you to talk to, to lean on, to confide in. You feel superhuman and at the same time, because you are a child and cannot fill that role as it should be filled, you feel inadequate. You're always a failure on some level. I don't know how my mother stood being visited by the husband who had withdrawn from her so long ago. I don't know how he visited the home of his wife whom he could only love from a distance, and in a pale and watered-down way.

My room was a space that was free from the eddies of pain and demand that swirled downstairs. I was allowed to design and arrange it the way I wanted to. When I was fourteen the shelves were filled with souvenirs, tchotchkes, music boxes and figurines. Everything changed when, at fifteen, I found the Zen Tea Garden room at the Philadelphia Museum of Art. I fell in love with the space, with white paper walls, green bamboo, and the sound of falling water. I boxed up all the tchotchkes and stuck them into the attic, except for a hollow white porcelain laughing Buddha figurine where I hid a joint someone had given me. I never had band posters up on the walls, I'm not sure why. If I had, it would have been James Taylor and Simon and Garfunkel, The Moody Blues and King Crimson. Led Zeppelin. I sat on the bed and learned songs by Joan Baez with the twelve-string guitar I'd asked for as a birthday present. It came with guitar lessons, which I ditched pretty quickly. That teacher wanted me to learn "The Bear Necessities" and I wanted to play "Bird on a Wire."

Not a member of the popular group, I liked the artsy girls, the girls with a little rebellion in their hearts toward the straight look, the straight body, the straight dominant girl-culture way of thinking. I was not drawn to the theater girls, who seemed to be always looking for a reason to chew the scenery. I know now that I would have adored the theater boys, but there were no boys at the school, so I had to wait for them until later in life. I loved the painters and the sculptors. The sculpture teacher was a sandy-haired man with a big mustache and a pink tie-dyed lab coat. From the time I set a cardboard box on fire while not paying attention during a welding lesson, he looked at me with a wary eye. The painting and drawing teacher, Ms. Fackenthal, had the best squint lines around her eyes, I imagined them being from walking around and looking at our work, and figuring out something both true and kind to say. Somehow at the same time she made me want to do better, to work with more patience and more attention. She really saw me. For our senior project we had to do a self-portrait. For some reason I chose a large canvas. Living with a twice-life-size picture of your own face when you are processing massive information about who you are at seventeen — you really see yourself. That was not all good.

Lisa

Part of what I was processing was about my sexuality. I'd been kissing Bill, my best friend's brother. I'd also been kissing Lisa, a girl in my class. She was the aggressor, but I'd been trained to be for people what they wanted me to be, which made me a bit of a go-with-the-flow person sexually. My ninth grade boyfriend, Steve, wanted to "do it" so badly that's almost all he talked about. I took the train into Philadelphia to see a doctor I'd found in the phone book. She examined me, said "I don't like to give the pill to girls your age," but she gave me a prescription anyway. I'm sure Steve did his best, but sex was underwhelming. Sex with Lisa at our sleepovers was better. She paid attention, and was interested in me. She'd grab me in the hall and pull me into an empty classroom, push me against the blackboard, and kiss me hard. My best friend Ellen found out. "She's a lesbian!" she said. I shrugged inside, but I was starting to think Lisa was a little too intense, and I wanted a break. Ellen told me I'd better not see Lisa any more. I have never been that obedient a person. I did grouse to Ellen about how aggressive Lisa was, and made it sound like the whole thing was her idea. Then Lisa disappeared.

What I found out later was that Ellen's mother had written a letter and sent it to the school, to my parents, to Lisa's parents, and I don't know who else. Lisa's parents yanked her out of school and took her to a psychiatrist. I never knew. I pretended I didn't care. One day when my children were in elementary school the phone rang. It was Lisa. We talked about what had happened. I apologized. She forgave me, for which I was and am grateful. She was still intense and a bit aggressive. I was worried for a while that she would show up at my door. She never did. She found Catholic Jesus some years later, and went on a different way.

I became less acquiescent sexually as I had experience with different people. One tenth grade boyfriend was a Unitarian Universalist. He was in something called LRY, which I didn't know anything about. I met his friends, and they were all the kind of kids my mother and father would worry about. Mama didn't like him because he was strange and intense, and because she called to the cat one day, "come out of there, stupid," and he answered to that. She felt that was not a good sign. He was a dramatic lover. When I broke up with him he said "I will kill myself this very night." Of course I didn't want him to, but all of my suicide-rescue energy was going to my dad, so I sighed wearily and said good bye, unwilling to be held hostage by someone else's emotional upset.

Spirit of Rebellion, Come *Out!*

༄

I started at Duke, lucked out with a roommate and professors, and tried to start liking beer. I never could, for some reason, so frat parties were not much fun. I would sit on the low wall of the frat house courtyard, and boys would sit down to talk for a minute. I didn't know how to flirt with boys. As the evening progressed, they got more and more drunk, until, in the middle of a sentence, they would fall off the wall. Forward or backward. Being sober in a group of people drinking, you don't get to enjoy the conversation. The things they find funny are mystifying. The stories the dedicated partiers tell all have to do with the last time they got drunk and something uproarious happened.

I majored in Political Science and Psychology. Later, when the show West Wing came on, I recognized all the characters I'd been in class with. Driven, fast talking, instant experts with little deeper understanding, "little picture" vision, hungry ambition. What I learned in both majors has helped a lot with the work I've chosen to do.

I fell in with the campus Christians very early on, went to Intervarsity meetings, and joined a Christian singing group, the JC Power and Light Company. There were about ten of us, and I was happy there. We sang a couple of songs I wrote, and that felt good. One, called "Soon Face to Face," was influenced by my father's longing for heaven. It was about how lonely the world was, how we were searching for the reason we were here and yearning to see God. Those weren't my feelings, they were my dad's, but I was just then getting separate from him, so we would no longer be pretty much the same person. I had a crush on a pre-med boy named Bob, a very serious Christian. The young woman I'd met first on the bus between campuses, Liz, had been talking to me about the baptism of the Holy Spirit, where people prayed for you to receive the gift of speaking in tongues, healing, knowledge, and other cool-sounding gifts. I told her I wanted Bob to be the one to lay hands on me. He came to my dorm room and we sat on the bed together. We prayed in the regular way for a few minutes, and then he took both my hands in his and started praying that the Spirit would come down. He prayed in tongues. It sounded strange, like listening to a radio station that had a rhythm but where you couldn't catch the words. After less than an hour I was ready to quit. He wasn't. He apparently had infinite patience for this part. My neck hurt. I was bored. So I started speaking in tongues, just to get him to stop and feel like he'd accomplished something. I don't guess that's the way it's supposed to happen, but it did the trick, and I did enjoy speaking in tongues over the next few years. It made my brain quiet and my head feel pleasantly empty. All of the "translations" of the strange tongues sounded the same, and you just had to shrug them off and not take anything too seriously.

A few of us from JC Power and Light wanted some more rock in our lives, so we formed an additional split-off band called "The Damascus Road Experience." We were loud, and toured a little and we had fans, and it was great. It was the first time I'd had young men as dear friends.

When I was twenty, a junior, I went to study Hebrew in Israel. My dad, the news man, had met the mayor of Jerusalem at a conference somewhere and they'd hit it off. He wrote to ask whether I could go to *ulpan*, a school for new immigrants in order to learn the language of their new country. He got me a place in the school, but I couldn't live there. I got a room at the YMCA in the Old City of Jerusalem, near King David Street. I walked everywhere, ate hummus and falafel, and had colorful dresses made for me in the bazaar. You could go into a shop, pick out your material from bolts and bolts on shelves, let a woman take your measurements, come back the next day and your dress would be ready.

The smell of the bazaar was my favorite thing. I sometimes get a whiff of it when I open my spice cabinet. Cinnamon, Turmeric, Nutmeg, Paprika, and chili are such a delicious mix of scents. Tea sellers would walk the cobblestone streets of the bazaar with a big brass jug of hot tea on their backs and a brass tray carrying tiny glasses attached by a strap to their waists. You could stop them and have a glass of tea when you needed refreshment. Pastry sellers had trays of sesame-studded pastries and sweet halva. Rugs and jewelry and cassette tapes of music were for sale, each in their own cubbyhole of a shop along the narrow alleyways. It was always crowded. Sometimes a man would be leading a donkey, laden with baskets holding round loaves of bread. In a larger passageway there might be someone leading a camel. Men would sit at the entrances to the shops, smoking. Some would smile and greet me. I would smile back, at first. Like any woman on any street in the world, you could make a pleasant face, but one in every so many men will treat that as an invitation, a commitment, almost. I learned to walk by and meet their greetings with a stony face. "Hey, smile," they'd call out.

Ulpan was fun. I fell in love with a mathematician from Romania, also with a Canadian photographer who lived in a house that was centuries old, so old that you had to climb down seven stairs to get to the white-walled courtyard. The street had been layering up with dirt and donkey droppings, with spilled tea and stones from people's shoes for 500 years. We picked hibiscus for tea from the small tree in the courtyard, adding juice from a lemon plucked from the lemon tree. The students learned folk dances, visited a Kibbutz, hiked in the Sinai Desert, climbed Mount Sinai, and floated in the Dead Sea, where the water is so salty you have to work hard to submerge your body. We snorkeled in the Red Sea and visited Masada.

On Spring Break I went on my own up to the Galilee, where I joined a tour of Pentecostal Christians. They invited me onto their bus and we ate St. Peter's fish, admired the red poppies carpeting the rolling hills, and walked around ruins being dug by archeologists. They were on their way to the Jordan

River, where there would be a baptism. I have a clear picture of the people from the bus, dressed in white robes, being dunked into the brown water, coming up out of the water, ecstatic, speaking in tongues. I had already been baptized, so I passed on that and watched from a little distance. The lady I sat next to on the bus had been excited about being baptized. I asked whether she'd been baptized before, and she said Oh yes, she did this every year.

I had moved from the Y into the home of a Christian couple who had moved to Jerusalem because Jesus was going to be coming back right there. She had a two-year-old boy and another on the way, and she was tired. I was supposed to clean house for her in exchange for my room. She was Dutch, though, and her idea of cleaning and mine were quite different. My mother was an indifferent housekeeper, and this woman was a devotee of scrubbing. Her husband was American, and they were kind to have me there. Hosting prayer meetings for the Charismatic Christians in Jerusalem was something they did often. We would sit in the living room in a circle, and tongues would be spoken and then interpreted. The interpretations all sounded pretty much the same: "My people, I love you. Obey my word. Hard times are coming." They all believed that the Tribulation was coming, and they were mostly "post-trib" believers. That means they thought that Christians would be persecuted and tortured before the Rapture came and we were all taken up into Heaven. Young people would sit around talking about what kinds of tortures they might be able to withstand. Me, none. All they would have to do would be to describe what they were going to do and I would crack.

The end for me with that couple came when I got back from the Sinai trip. She had thought I shouldn't go, that I should study instead. I was in Israel for my only time, and I wasn't going to study instead of having that experience. When I got back, my dad had sent me a fantasy book, the kind we both loved. *The Forgotten Beasts of Eld* was the title. I left it lying around in the living room one day and she read the blurb on the back, something about the woman on the front cover being a sorceress.

"Get this demonic book out of this house!" She demanded.

"My father sent me this book!" I objected. "I'm not throwing it away." They took me to a prayer meeting that night. A group of Pentecostal nuns from somewhere in central Europe were having an exorcism event near the Temple Mount.

"You have a spirit of rebellion," they said. At their insistence, I got in line to be exorcised. I saw the nuns praying with people, and then laying their hands on the people's heads and the people would fall down, "slain in the Spirit." They prayed the spirit of rebellion would leave me and when they put their hands on my head, they shoved. I took a step back. I thought "I'll be damned if I'm going to fall down when they shove me." Well, I'm not going to be damned, and I need that spirit of rebellion to stay close beside me.

Jesus Is Coming

As I've said, I've been working as a therapist since I was four. It doesn't take many times for a kid to hear that her dad has considered suicide for her to worry about keeping him alive. When he would cry at our weekly Saturday nights at the Philadelphia Orchestra, I would worry that he was thinking of dying. I think he told me first that, when he was a younger man, he'd contemplated driving his car into an abutment, just to end it all. My brain was so loud after he spoke that I'm not sure I remember it right. Big emergency flashers started and didn't really ever stop. Even in his nineties, he loved the idea of "flying," as he called dying. I've seen many folks in their nineties wish to be free of their failing bodies, and it's completely understandable. Romanticizing death in your forties or in your sixties, though, is hard on your children. He told me he married my mom because she wanted his life, and he didn't want it, so he might as well give it to her. That made no sense even then. I was ten. I think it would be easier if he hadn't confided in me when I was a kid that there had been times when he wanted to die. The ideation was often couched in religious terms, talking about Jesus' return. One evening I was cramming for a math test, and he said, cheerily, "Don't worry, Meggie, maybe Jesus will come back before the test and you won't have to take it!" I'm trying to view this with affection.

I understand wanting to die. There were times during my divorce when I was glad there wasn't a gun in the house. The guilt lay on me heavily. Sometimes a picture of my inner self would come to me. She was hunched over, head in her hands, and an enormous circular saw was descending toward her back. I was hurting my children, hurting a basically good man, all just for the selfish desire to be loved and to love with my whole self. When I called my dad to tell him I'd left my marriage, the first thing I said was "Now I understand why you and mom got a divorce." I was about to go on to ask him how it was for him, but then, "Well, I think you are doing exactly the wrong thing," he said, coldly. Whenever he shoved against my life with his Christianity, his neediness, his narcissism or his competitiveness with me, it always took me aback.

As a child I'd gotten used to him being by my side, but really, I was by his. I was part of him. Our conversations early on consisted of my asking "why"? and him being able to give lengthy answers (he always knew the answer) or his asking me a question, me saying "I don't know, what do you think"? and him answering at length. He is recently gone now. For the last three or four years he was in a wheelchair. His mind was sharp and his voice still beautiful as he read aloud. His wife is hugely kind, practical and strong, and they were devoted to one another. She'd been one of his students, quite a bit younger than he, and she held him in high regard. She loved him well, even though he was a complicated man.

By the end I was hardly ever blindsided by his reactions to things. I used to brace before I called, get my shields up, remember that I can trust him to be himself and no other. The same is true for me also, unfortunately. You can trust me to be myself and no other. When he was lying in a hospital bed with a heart problem, he was talking about choosing a cardiologist. "I asked the nurse," he said, "whether this man was a Christian. I knew he was from India, so he might have been a Hindu or a Muslim, and I wanted to make sure my doctor worships the same God I do."

"So you really think that God and Allah are two different and separate gods"? I asked, incredulous.

He started to give an answer about false gods, and his wife looked at me, and said, "Really, Meg, here? Now"? I subsided. We had fun arguing, my dad and I. For some members of the family, arguing theology is a sport. I remember having what sounded to me like a good conversation with my dad's sister Ruth about the femaleness of God. She was saying something about how God's energy is masculine because he penetrates the human world. "Might you just as well describe it as God surrounding the human world, taking it in to Godself? Would that be more a female energy"? She put her head in her hands and said she was too old to change her thinking on this. Suddenly we both looked in surprise at my sister, who had covered her ears and was crying.

"I just can't stand all this arguing!" she sobbed.

"But… we're having fun!" we told her.

"It's not fun for me!" she wailed, so we stopped.

I trust my sister to be herself. She can trust me to be myself, much as she might wish I would be a gentler spirit and push back less fiercely on the religion we grew up with. I can't change my spirit. I can change my behavior. I can try to be lovely and not push.

Here is what I learned. You can trust people. You can trust them to be themselves. Always. He was always going to be who he was. The dad who sent me to bed without supper when I was four, then sat with me and cried, holding my hand, until I fell asleep. The dad who explained everything from the absolute beginning of that thing, whose favorite question was "why"? The dad who took the stairs two at a time and was proud when I could match him stride for stride. Narcissistic, brilliant, manipulative, emotionally immature, adoring, competitive and cruel. I loved him, and I didn't anymore expect him to be the dad I would have loved to have had.

You Should Write a Book

❧

At the dinner table my mother would tell stories about the second graders in her class room. The stories were hilarious, and my dad would always say "Kathy, you should write a book."

Writing a book was the way, in my dad's family, to be somebody. The Big Man, the evangelist, had written many books. When I was a young Presbyterian minister, people would approach me often to ask "Are you related to Donald Barnhouse"? Usually it was the Big Man they were talking about. If I'd been his grandchild and a boy, I would have had no trouble being a famous Presbyterian minister in a "significant pulpit." I think that's what you'd call it. Anyway, I was a girl, which set the trajectory differently.

Aunt Ruth wrote books. She was a psychiatrist, the mother of seven children. Her life was marked, marred, by having been assigned Sylvia Plath as a patient when she was first in practice at McLean Hospital. They worked hard together, as you can read in the Bell Jar, but the tragedy of her death cast a shadow over Ruth. One of her books had to do with how homosexuality was a pathology for some reasons I didn't find out, as I wouldn't read those books. She meant for it to be kind, I think, but the book hurt a lot of people. My dad felt she was a bad influence. I was fascinated by her and grateful for her attention. Someone had given me a book about Kabbala, and she wrapped the book in brown paper, made signs over it with her hands, and we put it in the attic.

"Stay away from the Kabbala," she warned, "until you are over forty. Otherwise it will mess you up." She was a Personage, and she spoke in Pronouncements.

On my dad's side of the family, writing books is the way to be somebody. My Grandfather Barnhouse, the Big Man, had a radio show called The Bible Study Hour. He started a magazine called "Eternity." The way he preached was to work his way through a book of the Bible verse by verse, teaching with all his scholarship and devotion brought to bear on the passage's original language, on what the words meant in their time, on who the writer was and what he might have meant, and then what the meaning is for the people listening to him. The books which resulted from this practice are still carried in Christian book stores. My dad has written a couple of books, but was unwilling to be edited, so only one came out.

In seminary, my roommate Laurie was a journal writer. I bought a journal and became one too. After our studying was done we'd put on our long flannel nightgowns and write in our journals. It felt companionable, useful, important.

When my children were young I was working as a pastoral counselor. One night I got a phone call from a fellow named Pat Jobe. His name was familiar, but I couldn't place it. He'd gotten an assignment for a seminary class to talk to a minister who was serving in a non-parish setting, and asked if he could interview me. We talked for at least an hour and a half. We laughed and told stories and generally delighted ourselves and one another. Something about the combination of us made each of us lighter, funnier, deeper. He asked, toward the end of the conversation, whether I might like to write a commentary for his local NPR commentary series called "Radio Free Bubba."

"That's where I've heard your name. I love those commentaries!" I said, and I wrote one and took it up to the station in NC to record. They asked for more, and soon I was a regular.

"Make it three and a half minutes, make it funny and make it deep," they said. My first five books are collections of those commentaries. The first book, *Radio Free Bubba*, was a joint effort with Pat and Kim, the third commentator in the Bubba rotation, and my partner at the time. When Hub City published it, we began the world's longest book tour for one book. I think we went three years reading and singing. More about that later.

Skinner House, the UU press in Boston, published three of them and Hub City press in Spartanburg, SC published two. I put one out with my wife Kiya's publishing company. I've written two novels that have not been published, so I may put them out myself. Crown Books took one of them, but wanted a two-book deal, but I had two elementary school children and a job, so the second book took three years. By that time they'd moved on. Plus the second book had a lesbian couple in it, just as side characters, but that was still too much for my literary agent at the time.

As I've said, my father's side of the family has a little problem from time to time with being edited. When it was suggested that the Big Man get a PhD, he replied "But who would examine me"? I have been stiff necked about it once or twice, mainly when an editor from New England tried to take out the Southern phrases in my stories and replace them with Standard English, or when I quoted a woman who asked for a ride "to my brother house." She wanted to correct the woman's English. Why did she think replacing this Southern woman's words with "correct" grammar made the book better? I see the editor's dilemma, but here is the question: is it more respectful to honor the way the woman talked or more respectful to pretend that she spoke Standard English? Which choice lands on the side of love? I think I was fairly receptive in an un-Barnhouse way to her other edits.

Writing is the simplest thing in the world. You sit in the chair and you write words. You keep doing this and keep doing it whether you are inspired or not. You tell the truth as far as you are able. If you don't tell the truth the writing lacks juice, it lacks energy. When a piece of writing is bland, when your eyes skate over the words or your ears can't follow the sentences, it's because something is being glossed over. Obfuscated. Your anger should come through. Your hope, your cheesy delights, your frustration and care should come through, and if everything is not wrapped up in a neat bow at the end, that's ok. If there is no moral of the story, if you end with questions or musings or if the camera just pulls slowly back from the scene, it's going to be ok as long as it's the truth. Then you send your soul's truth out into the world, where it will not necessarily be treated gently. When I was sending hard copies of manuscripts out, one package of manila envelopes had a strip across the sticky part of the flap that said "Detach before mailing." Life-saving advice. The first few rejection letters seem to say "you are a terrible writer. You are ugly too, and probably should never have been born. Who do you think you are, anyway? Sincerely…" What they actually say is something like "thank you for sending this to us. Unfortunately, it does not fit our list." Detach from the outcomes, but not from the truth of your writing. It's tricky, but you just have to stand there with your little light shining through the high wind. I was wonderfully lucky, so eventually I got readers, and my readers wrote me back about the pieces or songs that meant something to them, and that has been more than enough to shore up my courage.

Seminary

ॐ

After a hiatus in writing from the age of ten to twenty-one, it began again because of my seminary roommate Laurie. As I've told you, she kept journals, and I loved her, and so I started keeping journals too. I would buy blank books and find a postcard, a picture that spoke to my soul, and paste it on the front, and then fill it with daily thoughts. In the evenings after our studying was finished, we'd write. There were things to figure out, faith questions, boyfriend questions, the friends who wanted to be closer than we wanted to be, the women in the classes ahead of us who were sure we wouldn't be feminist enough, and our own questions about whether we were feminist enough. Our writing escaped the journals and onto the walls of our room. A big quilt hung on one wall, and we would lift a corner of that quilt and write on that wall. We each had lists: Things I'm scared of. Things I need. Things I feel guilty about. The dorm was falling apart and bug-infested. It was to be demolished when we moved out, so we felt free to make the walls our own, breaking taboos by writing on the walls, by articulating fears, angers, guilts, hopes. Watching my words escape the journals felt like freedom. Soon we abandoned the safety of the wall behind the quilt and began writing everywhere.

I do think that, when a seed cracks open, it's probably feeling an uncomfortable combination of excitement and panic. That's how I felt in seminary as we began going in depth into the theology and history of my childhood faith. Suddenly everything cracked open. I was so angry at being fed "truths" that purported to be bread to feed your soul, but which, in fact, cracked my teeth as I tried to get them down. Christianity the way I was taught it is no place for a girl. Your body is unclean. Your will is dangerous. Follow your heart? Stupid girl. Your heart is deceitful. I was taught to ignore my instincts, ignore what didn't make sense to me. "God's ways are not our ways, His thoughts are not our thoughts," they said.

The Calvinist religion I was taught was based on the belief that we humans are miserable sinners, totally depraved in our nature. My problem was that I felt like a good person. I'd always tried to do what was right. At fourteen I was thinking about the Bible verse that says "If someone asks for your coat, give him your cloak also." My sister wanted a little decorative box I had, shaped like a chest of drawers. It was covered in a pretty Japanese cloth. I gave it to her, and I also gave her something else she didn't ask for. I don't remember what. It felt ok, but I felt more taken advantage of than I felt spiritual. She hadn't asked for the second thing, I'd just thrown it in, so it wasn't she who took advantage. I only blame myself and the teachings in which I was raised. That one example is no big deal, but there are thousands of times when I made myself act as if I believed something in order to be faithful. Faith, after all, is acting as if you believe something is true. The things that hurt me were the teachings about anger (don't be angry) the teachings about feelings (just be sweet) the teachings about sex (don't do it) and the teachings about femaleness (stupid, flighty, over-talking, weak, not leaders, second best). What strikes me now is that those teachings aren't really in the Bible. It says "be angry, but don't let the sun go down on your anger." That doesn't mean suppress it quickly before dark falls. I think it means deal with it. Go to the person at whom you are angry and try to work it out. I don't know. The teachings about sex are mean in the Bible. A woman who is raped must marry her rapist, if she is raped out in the fields where no one could hear her scream. If she is raped in town where she could have screamed, she is killed along with the rapist. If you have never read Leviticus, don't. It will curl your hair. The Bible certainly doesn't teach you to be sweet all the time. People were having feelings all over the place. Job and King David were yelling at God, Deborah was making battle plans and leading the people into skirmishes with enemies, people loved folks they weren't supposed to, rich men had wives and concubines, Abraham and Sarah lied and doubted and exhibited all sorts of family behavior we would count as dysfunctional. I think the religion I was taught was mostly "Churchianity," rather than Christianity. I'm not sure anyone has really ever practiced Christianity. It's too hard. Also, the whole story of the way God forgives sins made absolutely no sense to me. So he apparently sets up the world so people have free will. Then when they choose consciousness, the knowledge of good and evil, they are punished forever more. People are born into sin, I was taught. Little tiny babies, already sinners. I'll admit, babies are selfish buggers. They want what they want and they don't care who they bother, wake up, spit on, laugh at, get sticky, or stink out. Sinful, though? Nah.

They go on to teach that God killed his only son so he could forgive me. What?? Why not just forgive? Because there needs to be blood to cover sins, they say. That is the rule God made. Now this is a bit taboo to speak of, but don't many women bleed regularly without being hurt? He couldn't use that blood? He had to kill Jesus? My father disagreed with a lot of this. He was a free-thinking conservative Bible believer who wasn't up for all of that Calvinism. He put it like this. "If you owe me ten thousand dollars, I can forgive your debt, or your debt can be paid off. People teach that Jesus paid our debt of sin, and they also teach that, because of Jesus' death, God can forgive our debt. It can be one or the other, but not both. Is our sin forgiven or is it paid for"? Bravo to him, and I think he was right within that paradigm, but how is sin a debt anyway? Do I owe something to God when I wrong you? No, I owe you. I owe you an apology at least, amends, reconciliation. The whole thing has so many holes in it, I got exhausted trying to keep it all straight. In seminary I would have regular faith-breakdowns.

For years I've told myself that I loved seminary, every day of it. It surprised me when my wife recently asked me what *soteriology* meant. I looked it up to make sure I was telling her right, that it that it was the study of salvation, and then I burst into tears. I hate that fucking word. I hate that teaching, that we need saving. I know, you can see salvation as the path to wholeness, which is sweet, but not when you have to begin from the feeling that you are a miserable wretch. Maybe I just took all of it too seriously, but if you don't take it seriously you don't end up in seminary at Princeton.

I went there because it was where my mother and father had gone, where my grandfather had gone, where my uncles on my mother's side went. I guess Princeton was like Mecca for us Presbyterians. I moved into my single room in Erdman Hall and immersed myself in learning Presbyterian Christianity.

There was some variety in the student body. Some were international students, there were married and unmarried students, and a few women. Phyllis was already thirty, and she fussed over imaginary eye bags and wrinkles in the communal ladies' room. I think she was in love with one of the preaching professors. His name was Mc-something, and he'd spent a semester or two at St. Andrews in Scotland. He'd come back with a Scottish accent and hung on to it for the rest of his life. He had a little dog named Rory, and pronounced both "r"s with a burr on the tongue that we all tried to duplicate to make light of him.

Across the hall was a woman whose room smelled horrendous. She spent the afternoons making ice cream liquor drinks in her blender. I can't tell that she ever went to class. She was drunk a lot. And sad. I know she had her reasons. These were the main exceptions to the sweet, sincere, righteous, striving and kind students. That's not completely true. A lot of the male students (which was most of the students) were raunchy, joyously indulging in the sex and alcohol they figured they'd need to give up once they became ministers. At night, passing Alexander Hall, a men's dorm, you'd have to either put up an umbrella or give the fire escapes a wide berth. That's where they liked to stand to pee before going back inside to their Dungeons and Dragons game. The graduate students were the most fun. Val would come downstairs when he took a break from studying, place his Viking bulk in the doorway to my room and share a raunchy limerick. Here's the only one I remember, and I remember it particularly because my sister was visiting and I was embarrassed for her to so quickly lose her first view of what a seminary would be like:

'A woman from South Carolina / had fiddle strings 'cross her vagina. / With the right size of cock, / what was sex became Bach's / toccata and fugue in G minah"

The classes were fascinating: Greek, Hebrew, Church History, Theology, Pastoral Counseling, Religious Education, Preaching. The professors struggled to use inclusive language, not to use the word "man" for "humanity," not to talk about future ministers only as "men." This was the late

70s, and the few women who were a year ahead of us had made disruption of class their line of defense after talking reasonably to the teachers hadn't worked well. If a professor forgot, or relaxed into his realm of comfort and started using language that erased women, they would stand up and storm out. We didn't have to do that because the teachers were all afraid we would, so they tried hard. We knew it mattered, not only because we felt it deeply, but because studies were coming out which showed that when you use the word "man" to mean "humanity," people picture an actual man, as if that is the prototype human and woman is the other. Not man. There was an old riddle that still stumps some people. "A young man is rushed to the hospital by his father after a car accident. The surgeon says 'I can't operate on this boy, he's my son.' What's the story"? People twisted and turned to try to imagine — step father? Fugue state in a man who sees this boy and just thinks he's his son? The answer, of course, is that the surgeon is the boy's mother. When people hear "surgeon," they imagine a male surgeon. When people imagined "minister," they imagined a male minister. People would call us "women ministers." A more recent joke goes like this: "What do you call a woman pirate"? The answer is, in a pirate accent, "a pirate, you sexist dog!"

We fought for inclusive language because it was going to matter to our futures. If people didn't imagine women ministers, we would always be the other. Not the norm. Now most seminaries of protestant denominations are at least half women. The men worried aloud about that too. "If ministry gets too many women in it, it will go the way of nursing or teaching. It will become a woman's profession and we will lose status and salary." We would tell them that, for centuries, priests and ministers had been wearing long dress-like robes, holding babies, listening to people's problems, and serving bread to people. If that hadn't feminized the profession, they didn't need to worry about us.

Most of the few female students were reading feminist theology. We were reading it on our own. This was not an assignment for any class. We read "The Feminine Face of God," "The Chalice and the Blade," we read Mary Daly, Nancy Hardesty, and Virginia Ramey Mollenkot. We began experimenting with calling God "She." Sometimes we would alternate. The God we'd grown up with had never been presented as having female characteristics. We gathered all of the Bible verses that speak of God as a mother eagle, a hen, a nursing mother, and held them close to our hearts. Still, calling God "she" began to change me. If God can be "she," then I can feel myself more made in her image than I could before. Mary Daly said that calling God "she" had to be more than just dressing YHWH, the God of the Hebrew Scriptures, in drag. The characteristics and qualities of God begin to change. You imagine God differently and the world changes.

The women who went before us worried that we were not radical enough. They called us into a meeting room, into which all of the female students fit comfortably. They railed for a while about how being radical was necessary, and that if we wanted to run the Women's Center after they left we weren't going to be giving tea parties. Then they handed out boxes of matches to us. I'm not sure what all of that was about. My second-year roommate, Laurie, who was to be head of the Women's Center, was incensed, insulted. I guess I hadn't been paying good attention in the meeting. Laurie did well, I think. I remember fiery women speakers being brought to campus and great discussions about the feminist and then womanist theology we were reading. When people asked what it was like to be in that early wave of women in seminary, I tell them it was like trying to get over a tall electric fence. The first ones to throw themselves at it got fried, and the next wave of us crawled over their bodies to get to the other side. My listener invariably makes a face of distaste, and says something like "what a violent image!" Well, yeah. But you asked what it felt like. The average length of ministry for the women who graduated with me was three years. It was almost that bad for the men too. Ministry is a rough gig. This is my thirty-eighth year doing it, and I'm still engaged and interested, so it's the right livelihood for me.

You Should Get Married

꒰ꔛ꒱

I fell in love in seminary. My roommate had a kind of a crush on two men, fierce classroom-arguers. Mark had great shoulders and beautiful hands. He had a lovely voice, played guitar well, and was snarky-funny. We started hanging out. He wouldn't sleep with me before we were married. Weird, but ok. We sloped on toward marriage. I told him I was a lesbian, in all but sexual activity. I loved women, I was comfortable being around women, I'd had a lover in high school, and I wanted to live with women in a household. He countered, saying he could be a male lesbian, and we'd figure everything out like two women would. It worked for a little while. I loved him like crazy. He was just a slow-giving stream, barely able to squeeze out the words "I love you," even to our children. He grew tighter and more bitter year by year. I needed a big flowing river, someone who would speak and show their love daily. We were married for seventeen years and we have two handsome, funny and brilliant sons, so I ended up living in boy world, loving it, grateful. Just because a marriage ends doesn't mean it was a mistake. Relationships have a beginning, a middle, and sometimes an end. It's never all for nothing.

My roommate married the other guy.

I remember a conversation we had a couple of months before my wedding. "You know," I told her, "if one of us was a guy I'd want to marry you."

"Yeah," she said. And we moved on.

Not only did we like writing, she and I were both early-to-bed people. A few times we'd throw a party, and when the guests hadn't left by eleven, we'd put on our nightgowns. If they still didn't leave we'd run the vacuum cleaner and the party would move out to the hallway. In the afternoons we'd watch General Hospital. Mark would be studying in the other room, and every now and then he'd call out "Oh, Luke!" At the best times, there might have been six or seven people watching with us. This was before the whole show jumped the shark and Port Charles started sinking into the sea. I don't remember whether that was a literal plot point, but it sure does describe what happened to the show later.

I loved the classes, especially Church History, which was like reading old copies of People Magazine. I didn't enjoy Greek, but since I'd learned Hebrew already in Israel, I liked Hebrew class a lot. I aced the Bible knowledge test due to being raised with the Bible for breakfast, lunch, and dinner. In the middle year of the three, I became a Protestant seminary cliché, and lost my faith. Hard. I'd lie in bed, unwilling to get up to go to class. "But WHY did Jesus have to be killed? I'm not that sinful a person. I'm a pretty good person, actually. Couldn't God just have forgiven people without all the blood? Why did God make the world so that humans have free will to make bad choices, and then punish us for our bad choices? You wouldn't burn your child for doing anything wrong. Why would we worship a God who would burn his children for doing wrong"?

My fiancé Mark and my roommate would sit by the bed, holding my hands, and try to explain it all to me. "Listen, okay, we are all sinners and have fallen short of the glory of God," they would start.

"NoooOoooooOO!" I would wail. "That's such a set up!" We would all sigh.

Mama Dying

·ॐ·

It was around that time when my mother died.
She'd gotten breast cancer while I was away at
college. I was a sophomore when my step-
grandmother called to tell me that my mother had
been diagnosed with breast cancer. I don't know
why Mama didn't tell me herself. Maybe she was
worried that she would cry. That would have been
my reason, had it been me. The news was couched
in talk about the Lord and His will, and his healing
power, etc. My mind was so noisy I couldn't hear
her after the C word. It was serious, because
apparently she'd prayed about the lump for a year
before going to the doctor. I walked around in a
daze. What I wanted more than anything was to be
around people who were talking to each other, not
to me, where I could sit still and be blank and give
my noisy brain a rest. She had chemo. Her hair fell
out. She wore an ill-fitting wig. Missionary kids
don't buy the best for themselves, even if they can
afford it. She stayed cheery. "Meggie," she told me,
"everything that happens to me is good, because it's
from the Lord."

She invited a young Japanese woman to live
with her, Harumi Suzuki. Harumi was a student at
the Bible College in Philadelphia, and she took care
of Mama. I will forever be grateful to her. Mama
had told me to go on and continue school rather

than come home to take care of her. That was generous, and it's what I would have done for my kids, I hope. I still don't know if staying in school was the right decision, though. How do you ever know whether a decision you've made is perfect? Maybe there are no perfect decisions. We do our best with what we have at the time. Maybe there are two or three good decisions to go with any situation, or maybe there are none. Harumi was kind to my sister and me when we were there to visit, and didn't give any guilt or shame to us. She was glad to have a wonderful Christian lady to take care of and a place to live in exchange for loving care. I wish I knew where she is now.

My mother constantly sought a reason for her cancer. Maybe she needed to stop drinking coffee. Maybe she needed her back adjusted. I used to think it was the sorrow and pain of her marriage and the divorce. Having had cancer now, a little case, a tiny case, I think making up reasons for illness is blame-y and wrong. A human body is part of nature. Nature has blights. Sometimes a body gets sick. Maybe it's no more than that. Who knows? A faith healer told her she had cancer because of an unconfessed sin in her life. This sweet second grade teacher who loved her students and stayed with her difficult husband and reared us with kindness and every attempt at uprightness — she had an unconfessed sin? She believed him, though, and searched her heart and her history to find some sin that remained unconfessed. She twisted herself up over it. I feel anger and sorrow imagining worshipping a God who would sit, arms crossed, looking down at you, saying "I could heal you, but I won't because you have an unconfessed sin in your life. You have to purge your system of every imagined slight, large or small. You have to sit here under this bright light, tied to this chair, and tell us everything you know and then we'll think about letting you live. That doesn't sound like a God of Love or Mercy, or even Justice. It sounds like a Gestapo God, and I'm not happy that she was more willing to imagine a Gestapo God than to believe that nature had brought cancer to her mortal body and God would walk with her through it, kindly, with warm and supporting hands.

One night, my second year in seminary, she called. Sounding faint and far away, she said "Meggie, I think the Lord is taking me."

"I'm coming," I said. A lovely student named Sue was in the hall. I told her what was happening, and she offered to drive me the hour and a half home. I remember being in the passenger seat of her car, watching I 95 flow by, the night, the headlights, the silence. She didn't try to talk. I didn't talk. My mother's sister Edith was there, and my sister. I dragged a mattress downstairs so I could sleep by the couch where Mama lay. She was spitting up dark bile, so we cleaned that up and changed her nightgown. Drifting in and out of lucidity, she would say my name once in a while. She could talk to all of us. "Let's read the Bible," my dad said.

NO! I said, let's just be here with her. I was tired to death of this family using the Bible as a filter and a shield from all human experience, as if it were truer than life. Of course I didn't say that out loud, as it would have caused much hurt, much wailing and gnashing of teeth, to use a phrase, well, from the Bible. We talked to her and around her. They went to bed and I lay down on the mattress next to her couch. Late at night, I felt her stir, and I called her name. "Just a minute, I'll be right there," she said softly, as if coming back from being away. She died early that next morning, January eleventh.

The ministers were called, the funeral home was called. My father and I went to get a casket. We refused the teak walnut fancy thing. Tenth Presbyterian had a policy that all caskets be covered by a shroud belonging to the church, so no one had to compete to show how much they loved their deceased relative by spending the most money on the casket. We picked out the one they used for cremations, much to the disappointment and disapproval of the funeral guy. We were tough, though, having talked about death of the body many times over dinner, on car rides, etc. We knew what we thought, that she wasn't there anymore, and that she'd gone to join God. The funeral was awful. The Messianic Jewish assistant minister of my grandfather's old church, Tenth Presbyterian Church, in downtown Philadelphia, preached the funeral, and gave an altar call, which is just not a very Presbyterian thing to do. I don't know why we didn't have the funeral at our little church in Valley Forge. I think we'd gone less and less as she was on her journey with the faith healers, searching for an unconfessed sin in her life. The minister who ran off pamphlets in the basement would not have supported those shenanigans. The best part of the awful funeral was when we sang "For all the Saints," which to this day makes me cry.

I didn't go to the graveside in Doylestown. I don't know why she was buried there next to the Big Man and the step-monster. I regret that decision, made because I was angry that my dad had taught me my whole life that death was nothing, and that dying was just like having a shadow pass over you, and that it's a person's life that mattered, and now he was trying awkwardly to shame me into going to the graveside. "It might be bad for your career," I think he said, "People won't understand." F that. F all of it. I went to the airport to catch my flight to California, not in the best shape to meet Mark's parents. All my life I have given myself little gentleness, little care. I've treated myself as if I were super-human. Anyone else would have changed her plans, at least given herself time to grieve. The wedding was in May, and this was January, and my roommate said I couldn't marry Mark without meeting his parents, so I went, heartbroken and numb.

I've sat with a number of dying people since that night Mama died, and it always feels like an honor. Reality expands, as if this is one of the most real things there every will be. Listening to someone's breath slow, then stop, while family and friends are gathered, holding hands, touching the feet of the beloved person, is a moment of deep holiness. I don't know what happens when we die. No one does. No one does. Some believe we are met on another plane by people we've loved. I've seen people who are dying talk to folks they knew in life, as if beloveds are gathering to welcome them over. When my great grandfather was dying, the family had come together. Some of them were sitting on the front porch. Through the open windows, they heard him say "Isaiah, I'm James Hearst Pressly from Statesville, North .Carolina. Good to meet you. Jeremiah, I'm James Hearst Pressly from Statesville, North Carolina. Good to meet you." I would like the meeting of beloveds to be true. My hesitation lies in the thought that most of the people I'm related to who have gone before would not probably like or approve of me. Maybe they get broader, instantly or slowly, as they spend a longer time dead. I'm hoping that happens. Then they might gather around to welcome me without tightened mouths about my lack of faith or my lovely wife Kiya. Or maybe the folks I'm kin to in spirit and thought will be there instead: Audre Lourde, Maya Angelou, Boadicea, and maybe Mark Twain will gather around. Or they might disapprove of me for other reasons. I'm realizing as I write this that I expect disapproval from people I admire. I'm not radical enough, not smart or cool enough, too white, too clueless, too blind to my own blind spots. Maybe I disapprove of myself, at the root of things. I hope as I lie dying, or afterwards, I can broaden enough to welcome myself into the mystery with love and peace. I hope I'm surrounded by love, as the people I've sat with have been, as my Mama was. And whether she still worries about me or not, I hope I get to throw my arms around her again.

Being Born a Girl

❦

Being born female affected everything about seminary, from the first day to graduation. On the first day, a young man began confronting the few women in the dining hall, asking us belligerently to defend our sense of call to the ministry. He drove a red sports car with California vanity plates that read REVRICK

When you are born a girl, for clothes you get colors, textures, skirts that twirl, socks with rainbow stripes, shoes with lights or sparkles. I loved all of these things, or would have, if they'd all been invented when I was a girl. When you are born a girl your looks get lots of comments. Your hair, your clothes, your size, your skin, your hair clips or ribbons. People have patience with your tears. Sometimes an exasperated parent will say "I'll give you something to cry about!" but if you're a girl there is no horrified recoil from your emotionality. The main emotion that's off limits to you, anger, is pretty much the only one that's commonly allowed to boys. When you're born a girl you are told to be ladylike, which usually means being quiet and sweet. Keep your knees together, don't spread out, don't wave your hands around, and keep your voice down. Much of this, I'm sure, is particular to WASP culture, which is the one I grew up in, and I can't pretend to know much about anybody else's. My mother told me not to beat boys at games, to let them talk, to "draw them out," not to let them feel I was too strong, solid, willful, angry, skillful, or opinionated. Being raised a Southern girl gives you extra in this department, because you also have to be pert and entertaining, a good story teller, hospital visitor, Sunday School teacher; you should be musical, charming, know what to do with cut magnolia leaves on the mantel, and make everyone happy. The reality in my mother's family was that the women managed all of this while still being vivid characters. The husbands held their own, at least a few of them did, telling wild tales about tricks they had played on each other and that enormous Santa Gertrudis bull their daddy had brought from Texas, which was simply too big for North Carolina. Uncle David had sunk a concrete pillar into the ground with an iron ring on top. He chained the bull to the ring, but the morning light revealed the bull grazing far down into the pasture, dragging the concrete pillar behind him as if he barely noticed it.

When I was pregnant for the first time, I wondered what would happen if kids didn't get identified as a girl or a boy so soon, but I don't know how that could happen. I tried dressing my baby sons in yellow, letting them play with whatever they wanted to play with except guns. I didn't even mention guns. They liked to play fast and rough, they liked decibels, and would make any space they inhabited louder. They liked seeing how things moved and whether they could stop them moving. Or take them apart. Or make them move faster. When they did discover guns at a friend's house, they were transfixed. Video games were their passion as they grew older. My younger son learned to read early so he could put in the cheat codes for the games. I let them have shooting games later, but only if there were female characters who did their own fighting. There could be no rescuing of princesses and no actual shooting of human figures.

I know there were girls who were fast and loud, who liked shoot 'em up video games, but I didn't know any back then.

Then, in every girl's life, there's The Bad Man. A girl's childhood is always tinged with the knowledge that there are bad people who want to do bad things to you. When I was ten, in the bedroom with the ballerinas and the horses, there was a closet with sliding doors. That's where coat hanger monster man lived. He was very thin, so thin that when he was turned sideways he blended in to the clothes hanging there. At night I would dream that he slid out from the line of clothes and turned face forward, white, white skin, a sharp nose, blond hair cut short and slicked back, cold blue eyes. He wore a blue and white checked bathrobe. He terrified me, but I knew he was only in fearful dreams.

I would say that it was around the age of fifteen that I was convinced to be afraid all the time. My cousins and I agreed that it felt like there was a rapist assigned to us, that if we didn't do everything right he would attack. Even if we did do everything right. Before I was fifteen I would walk in the woods alone, exploring, poking around in fallen logs and in the ruins of an old church on the property of a large estate near my house. When Mama took us to Avalon, New Jersey for a summer vacation, I would walk on the beach alone at night, making my mother worry. "What if a bad man comes across you on the beach"? she asked, hesitant to spread fear, but wanting to do her due diligence as a mom.

"He won't be able to see me in the dark, Ma," I said.

"What if he has a flashlight"? she countered.

"He won't be able to catch me. I'll run fast."

"What if he has ropes to tie you with"?

"Ma," on my way out the door of the big rental beach house, "how will he catch me all weighed down with a flashlight and ropes"?

I don't remember when I began to accept the fear I was supposed to walk around with.

Boys do get attacked, but I think they are not taught to fear walking alone at night the way girls are. Women who were born presenting as males — were they afraid of being attacked when walking alone before they presented as women or just since they transitioned? Do they enter into the realm of female fear, or were they there before because of feminine qualities? So many women are killed by lovers and partners. How many are killed simply because they've entered into the female-presenting group of humans, where three of us every day are murdered by husbands or boyfriends? I know some trans folks are killed because of trans phobia. I feel all of us as vulnerable, out in the world in our thin skins and fierce hearts.

At times I'm glad that some of my women friends assigned "male" at birth did not get "the training" I got as a little girl. I shrug off some of the ways women are spoken about, the ways women are treated. Women I know who were raised as little boys get madder, in my limited experience. They grew up being treated as male, and they don't see a reason to get shabbier treatment now that they are presenting as the women they are. I watch in admiration as they take on "the way things are." What gifts can men who were raised as little girls bring to the world? I look forward to the richness and layering of perspective the trans community can bring to the world when they reflect on their experiences.

Being born a girl meant you were not going to be hired by a Presbyterian church, in those days. Near graduation was job interview time. I interviewed with senior pastor after senior pastor. "Will you be willing to do Christian Education Director jobs"? they all wanted to know.

"I didn't take any classes in that. I was a Preaching major," I said.

"That's what I do," they would say. "Why would I hire someone to do what I already do" Now, from having been a senior minister for years, I do understand their point of view.

One congregation asked me to drive down to the very end of New Jersey, Cape May, to interview with them. My roommate came with me. It was sleeting and the roads were icy. It took us two hours to get there. We all talked well together, and I thought it had gone well. At the end, they said "Well, our congregation isn't ready for a woman, but the Presbytery said we needed to interview a certain number of women, and we really wanted to meet Donald Barnhouse's granddaughter. Good luck going home!"

The Presbyterians were struggling to get churches to look at hiring women. My roommate got a job with the Presbytery of Pittsburgh as a circuit riding preacher who was paid to preach in churches all over the area just to show them what it was like to have a female in the pulpit. She was received politely. The standard communication from the ministers was "I would love to hire a woman, but my congregation isn't ready." Sometimes she would finish preaching and men would come through the line, joshing with her. "You didn't scream or throw up or fall down or anything!" It's a stretch to take that as a compliment.

Being born a girl meant you married boys. And I loved that boy Mark, and he promised to try to be in the marriage differently, like a girl, so I married him. We had our wedding in Miller Chapel. Friends made food, friends did flowers, and the minister from Valley Forge married us. My father came, along with beloved teachers and supervisors. Aunt Ruth told Mark he'd better treat me well, because we were all witches. "I think I can treat her well without threats," he said, coolly. A vintage convertible drove us down Nassau Street. We honeymooned in New Hope. Mark brought a John Updike novel, and the honeymoon was awful and awkward.

A few days later we were driving to Springfield, Missouri so I could do a summer internship at a Presbyterian church there. Mainly what I remember about the drive was looking out the window and thinking about throwing my wedding ring out into the fields, then taking off on foot to go be a waitress somewhere. I kept the ring on. The job was supposed to be for six weeks, and I was looking forward to learning from the minister. He greeted us with his family already in the packed car, headed out of town for a six week vacation. He had neglected to tell me that I would be the only minister there for the summer. The people were lovely, though, and mostly helpful. One lady called me every morning at seven because her husband, an Elder in the church, was having an affair with one of his students. I called the minister on vacation to ask what to do. He said not to answer the phone, and to call her back at a time that was more convenient for me. There is almost no emergency that won't keep for a couple of hours, he advised. I asked what I should do about the husband, who was still an Elder, and would be serving communion in a week or two. Should I tell him he couldn't do that?

"Well, Meg," he said, "it's a think (thin?) dime that doesn't have two sides. Would you want to be married to her"? I told him I hadn't asked her to marry me, but he had. He told me to do what I thought was best. Sink or swim, Baby.

When that internship was over we went traveling with Eurail Passes, and it was a wonderful trip. We had the same traveling style, which was to stay in one town for a week or so, read lots of books, drink wine and eat bread and cheese in the parks, and walk everywhere. We came back the night Reagan was elected.

We got some house-sitting jobs that year while I looked for work. Overstuffed dusty houses of lovely liberals whose dining room tables were piled with appeal letters from good causes, one amazing mansion on Battle Road where the folks had gone to Palm Beach for "the season."

We ate bagels with cream cheese on Sundays and read the New York Times instead of going to church. I kept watching the seminary jobs board.

Converse

୬୨ର

Finally a job in SC was posted. A women's college was looking for a chaplain, and they wanted to hire a woman. My husband and I eagerly looked on a map to find Spartanburg, SC. He said that since he was more marketable than I, having a penis and all, we should get me a job and then he would find something nearby pretty easily.

We took the Southern Crescent down for the interview and pulled in to the station at four in the morning. Groggy from sleeping sitting up, I was not doing well in the first interview. The no-nonsense dean of students, a former gym teacher, handed me a Coke and said "Drink this." I owe her whatever success I had that day. The sugar and caffeine did their job. The interviews were endless. Lunch with the faculty was fun. Dinner with the students was great. We did our imitations of a faith healer named Ernest Ainsley, who always asked someone he'd "healed" from deafness to "Say baby! Say baby!" I found out later that they almost didn't hire me, but the students' opinion that I was the best won out. The main problem the adults had with me was that I had a different last name from my husband. Apparently one of the deans made a pilgrimage to Plum Street to the home of the Chairman of the Board of Trustees. He confided, worriedly, the true fact of my last name and waited for the verdict.

Apparently Big Walter was okay with it, and gave the go-ahead. I had a job! In the Presbyterian Church, you didn't get ordained until you got a specific job, so it was time to plan my ordination.

Ordination

I set my ordination for the evening of Pentecost Sunday, 1980. Pentecost's liturgical color is red, so I had ordered red balloons for the sanctuary at Valley Forge Presbyterian Church. In Princeton, getting ready, my friend Laurie was consulting on the outfit. I pulled out a navy blue skirt and a gray silk blouse. The room was small. She was sitting on the bed and I was pushing hangers apart on the rail to get to the ones I wanted her to consider. This was the room I'd lost my faith in every six months.

Laurie looked at the gray blouse and the navy skirt and said, "Those are lady minister clothes. We're ordaining you. The real you. Here, wear this." She pulled out of the closet a dress I'd gotten in Istanbul, red, with embroidery on the front and tiny mirrors that caught and scattered the light. I was shocked. Then I realized she was right. The red dress it was. She spoke at the service, what we call the "Charge to the Minister."

"Don't compromise yourself to fit into people's views of what a lady minister should be. You are a minister of the gospel, and you will preach and you must stand up tall and say the words the spirit gives you. Don't compromise. Even if you do, no one will notice, and it will cost you. And them." I bless her forever for that.

In ordination, the teaching of my church at the time was that you were ordained to a certain job, the job of being a minister in some capacity. You don't get ordained to just be an ordained person. That doesn't make any sense, as if some powers are conferred on you that others don't have. You don't walk around in the world more capable of bringing down a blessing from the skies or changing bread into flesh. Your ordination says you have been educated and equipped to do a job for the church, for the people in the church. You are trained in pastoral counseling, teaching, worship planning, creating moments where people are invited to connect with The Holy and with one another. With my roommate Laurie's help, with Joe and Esther Jensen's help, the minister of my home congregation and his wife, with red balloons and a red dress and the power of Pentecost all around us, hands were laid on me in the ancient way, to confer on me collegiality, encouragement, companionship and accountability as a brand new minister.

According to the Christian faith story, tongues of fire sparked over the heads of the disheartened disciples as they gathered after Jesus' death. They began speaking in other languages, not the same one. In my preaching life I have stayed true to this Pentecost moment. Even as I lost my orthodox Christian beliefs, I spoke in my own language, which was understood by the people who heard me. Telling the truth as I saw, felt, and believed it was what led me to let go of the Christianity I'd been taught. Having been ordained, not as lady-minister-mè, but as me, the real me in my most travelled, decorated, joyous, and faintly rebellious mode, has meant everything. Giving life to my sense of ministry, being centered in the Spirit of Truth and Love, I feel its flames playing above my head from time to time.

You're Not from Here

※

My office at the college was on the second floor of the library, with a big window looking out over one of the quads. I sat in there in my black tights, corduroy jeans jacket and clogs and looked out at the students in their pink and green outfits, circle pins, careful hair and cute sweaters. People could just look at me and tell I was from Somewhere Else. "You're not from here, are you"? was a question I heard often those first years. I think I didn't stick out as far as the years went by, but it could be that people just got to know who I was.

I'd grown up in North Carolina, so I understood the accent, mostly. Still, I had trouble in the checkout line a couple of times when the cashier said "Got a pin"?

"Excuse me"?

"Got a pin"? A little irritated now.

"I'm sorry…" and I was.

"A ANK PIN!" she fairly shouted.

"OH!" I produced an ink pen.

"You're not from here, are you"?

At the hardware store I was returning a weed eater that had never performed well. The man behind the counter looked at it, lying on the Formica between us.

"Jemty dawl at"? he asked. I could tell it was a question because his voice rose in tone at the end of the sentence and he was no valley girl.

"Excuse me"? I said.

"JEMTY DAWL AT"? he said louder.

"I'm sorry," I said, and I was.

"Did you. Empty thawl. Out"? OH! Did I empty the oil out!

"No, I didn't. I don't have a place to do that safely." I said.

He gave me a disgusted look. "You're not from here, are you"?

After fifteen years, I was from there. My children are from there. It was a good town to raise children in. The town got better and better. A coffee shop opened downtown. Three people in the crew I had coffee with there every morning started a publishing company called Hub City. The first book was a gorgeous coffee table book celebrating a sense of place. The town used to be called "Hub City," because of the train, including the one I'd first arrived on that early morning long ago. They asked twelve or thirteen writers and twelve or thirteen artists to create pieces for the book that evoked a sense of place. I was proud to be one of the authors. It was a great success. The textile mills had shut down, and the town had been in the doldrums, searching for its identity. This book gave the town a sense of itself as being full of writers and artists, which it was. The book launch party was at the old train station, and it was attended by a crowd of proud people. More books followed, including *Radio Free Bubba* and the *Best of Radio Free Bubba*, two books I'm a big part of, and now Hub City Press is one of the foremost independent literary presses in the South. I'm not nearly literary enough for their list now, but I sure am proud to be from there.

A mayor was elected who'd read the book about Cultural Creatives, and he formed a "Blue Jeans Committee" to make the town cooler still. They renovated an old shoe warehouse and put the Hub City offices on the second floor along with an art space and listening room. A fancy restaurant went in on the first floor, and on the third floor were studio/living spaces for artists who would apply from around the US to come live free for a year and interact with the community through their art.

New people began to move to town, and I began offering unofficial orientation lessons to people who weren't from there.

"You'll think because the language is the same that you are still in the same culture you came from, but you are not," I would tell people who took me up on my offer. "Here, people will smile and look kind and cheerful all the time when they are talking to you. You may think it's fake, but it's not. It's a real dance of communication that just has different steps from the one you might be used to. For example, you have to listen to the tone of the words, as you would if you were listening to Chinese, another tonal language. There are different meanings depending on the tone. People will almost always say 'yes' to you, because it would be so rude to say 'no,' but you have to tell from the tone of the 'yes' whether it's a yes or a no. If you invite someone to a dinner or a party or an event, and they say a cheerful 'We'll try!' That's a no.

"Here's another thing. If they ask you if you'd like some tea, for example, and you say yes right away, that's rude. You have to say 'no, don't go to any bother.' They'll ask again, and you say no again in some nice way. If they never wanted to get you any damn tea, they'll leave it there. If they really don't mind, they'll ask a third time, and then you say 'why yes, that would be great.' Three times is the way people will ask if they really want you to come over for a visit, etc. If they only say one time 'Y'all come see us sometime!' that's just a dance of politeness. Don't go see them."

Those are the intro basics. The dance is formal and imbued with layers of meaning. It takes time to master. Pretend you just moved to Japan and you are learning the rules about bowing, business cards and subway riding.

Yeah, I've got an ank pin. I'll be happy to lend it to you. No, really, I'd be delighted. No? Ok then.

Converse 2

༉

I loved my work as the Chaplain to that college. It was the true Deep South. It hadn't been too many years since the students had been required to wear white gloves when going off campus into town. Daughters of magnates and captains of business mingled with young women of more modest means. Some were quick, full of light and intelligence. Others were a little dimmer, but the college made room for them. I was asked to teach in the religion department. Later I taught public speaking. Human sexuality was a course I was asked to teach. I'm not sure how that happened. I taught it peacefully for a few years until the semester when I drew the male and female genitalia on the blackboard and said, offhandedly, "If you don't know what you look like, I'd suggest you get a mirror and look." Months later I was called in to the Office of the President.

"I've heard rumors about you," he said. He'd always been kind to me. His mother had been a Christian Science Reader, so women in ministry were familiar, if not dear, to him.

"What are they saying"? I asked.

"Well, it's about an assignment you gave in your Human Sexuality course." He shifted awkwardly in his big chair. "Some students of Don (can't remember the last name of the far right uber

Christian music professor) say that you assigned the class to masturbate in front of the mirror for an hour and then write a paper about it." My jaw dropped. "I know it's not true, because I know you. The best way to fight a fire is to light a back fire, do you know what I'm saying"? He looked at me. I had no idea.

"Not really," I said.

"You tell the story before they can. Tell your story. The real one, and then people will have already heard that when the rumor comes around." So I did. I started laughing about the story with friends and acquaintances.

One friend said, "Oh, I heard that one! I was showing a friend pictures from the baby shower, and they gasped when they saw you in one of them. 'That's Meg Barnhouse!' she said. 'We're praying for her in our church.' I asked her why, and she told me what they'd heard about your Human Sexuality class. I knew it couldn't be true." Here is one thing I appreciate, because it's rare. Usually when someone hears a rumor or an accusation, they go to the middle, imagining there is truth on both sides, not wanting to decide who is in the right. It means a lot when someone doesn't go to the middle, when they know that what they just heard is silly BS.

In the Women in Religion course, I assigned the students, just for the six weeks of that Jan-term class, to refer to God in their classroom conversations and in their papers, as "she." I suggested this could begin to balance five thousand

years of the Jewish and Christian tradition calling
God "he" exclusively. "I could NEVER call on a
female God," one young woman said, "that God
would be too weak to help me." That told me
something about her and her family. One student
came to my office, angry, and told me it was very
unfair of me to force them to think about God in
this way. I told her how happy I was that the
exercise was raising up feelings of such passion in
her. That's was it was for, and perhaps she might
examine her inner resistance and outrage and learn
something. Another student reported that, telling
her parents about the class assignment in a
restaurant, she noticed a waitress sponging off the
table behind them, slowly, listening. When they got
up to go, the waitress stopped her and said, "Honey,
if you keep on doing that, you'll go straight to Hell."

Shelter

๛

In the first year of living in South Carolina, I saw a little announcement in the classifieds in the Spartanburg paper asking if there were anyone interested in helping to start a shelter for battered women in our town. The United Way had funded an organizer to help start shelters in three South Carolina counties, including ours. I called the number and went to the first meeting. The organizer was there, of course, joined by a thirty-something social worker, and I was the third. The social worker said she was there because she dealt with so many abused women, but that she was burned out. She didn't have much energy for the project. I was twenty-six, and I said "I'm not burned out."

I couldn't believe there wasn't a shelter in any of the three counties already. The organizer said she'd started at the police station, where she was told there was no problem with spousal abuse in this area. We started an organization called SAFE Homes, Shelter Available for Emergencies. It began with private homeowners recruited to house a woman and her children in an emergency situation. When we had about five homes ready, we put the word out with social workers that this was available. The calls started coming. We'd pick a place to meet the woman where she felt safe. This was not at her home. It would be a park or the library or some neutral location. I remember being chased, a woman and child in my little Honda. "He's got a gun!" she screamed. We drove to the police station parking lot and he drove on by. I had the thought that maybe this was not the smartest way for me to spend my one wild and precious life. Because of incidents like this, the police worried about us, the volunteers, the drivers, the homeowners, so they would help occasionally. The United Way funded a director for the organization, which grew quickly. The woman we hired was fierce and talented, and, in the four years I served as President of the board, SAFE Homes grew, bought a building for the shelter, and put down roots in the community.

Pegasus

༄

I applied for a faculty development grant to study dream analysis with a Jungian who lived in the mountains just over the North Carolina border.

At our first phone call, Polly, the Jungian analyst, told me that I should pay attention to any dream I had the night before we met. It could hold guidance for us as we began our sessions. Polly had agreed to teach me for a summer, using my own dreams. Her home was on a ridge in the North Carolina mountains. It was made of cedar wood, so it smelled wonderful. Her huge Bernese Mountain Dog, Riggi, snuffled me and then flopped down by Polly's chair. Often during that summer's work, if I got sad about something that came up, Riggi would heave himself to his feet and come lean on my knees. That first day, Polly raised her eyebrows at me and asked whether I'd dreamed the night before. I had. "I was riding on the back of a white winged horse," I told her. "We were following a deep gorge, flying over its deepest part. Bridges connecting the two sides of the gorge flashed by under us,. The wind in my hair and the warm solid body of the horse under me felt both safe and powerful."

"Let me ask you some questions," she said. "Every part of the dream is you. Is there a deep gorge in you, a divide between two parts of your inner landscape"?

"There is at least one," I answered. "My faith and the faith I was born into, my body and my mind, things I'm supposed to believe and things I actually believe. There is a lot of integrating to do."

"Well, you're not going to do it the regular way. That is what this dream seems to be saying. There are bridges that connect the two sides..."

"Plenty of bridges," I agreed.

"You're not going to use any of them. You're flying over the gorge itself, perpendicular to the bridges. Lots of ways across, but you're following the gorge itself as your way. Now, do you have a flying horse in you"?

"Um..." No one had asked me that before. "I have always loved horses. They've given me delight, taught me responsibility, given me power, and hurt me badly. I limp because a horse I didn't know jumped the side of the ring instead of the jump we were supposed to be going over."

"So, this one is going to be all those things in you. Your power, your strength, your care for beings, and your vulnerability. You know it can hurt you, but this one is flying. If that other horse could have flown, you wouldn't have fallen hard because it wouldn't have landed, maybe"? I was nodding. "You're going to use all those things as you fly along this division in you. Not using the bridges to go back and forth, just flying above and along the gorge.

"This is a significant dream, as you had it the night before we met. It tells you about a theme for your life, or at least for this work we're doing together." That felt true. I went home and read up about Pegasus, and learned that he is the child of Poseidon, the sea god, and Medusa, with her fearsome face. With his hoof print he created a fountain, sacred to the Muses, whose waters bring forth poetic inspiration.

We laughed a lot. I told her one day I thought I might be going blind. In my twenties I was ready for anything to go wrong, I don't know why. She laughed and asked if I'd cleaned my contact lenses lately. No I hadn't.

She told me about a client who, after months of dream work, finally confessed that he never remembered his dreams; he'd just been making them up. She told him it didn't matter one bit. His imagination was how his unconscious was talking to him. They continued to work on his made-up dreams.

I looked forward to the hour's drive to her home, to the views over the Blue Ridge, to Riggi and Polly's wisdom, the smell of cedar, the big loom in the main room. In addition to learning that everything in the dream was me, I learned the importance of the feel of the dream and the emotions within it. I'd been reading Jung since college, but I went back to it, and to the books written by his students and friends. Mostly, in my counseling practice which came a few years later, I used regular Family Systems theories, but now and then I'd work with a client's dreams. I have used mine for guidance throughout my life.

I knew it was time to leave my college chaplain job when I dreamed I was graduating in a cap and gown, walking across the college's stage and accepting my diploma. I knew not to take a job at a downtown church when I dreamed I was a waitress in a restaurant filled with people from that church. They were snapping their fingers at me, treating me scornfully.

At a time when I was struggling with whether to end my marriage, I dreamed that I was in a university room with a Gothic window high in one wall. Suddenly one of my favorite authors, Robertson Davies, was with me, and gestured to a ladder, which we climbed. We reached the window and sat together on the sill with our legs dangling over the outside stone wall. I looked behind me and the ladder had disappeared. I didn't know how to go back. He gestured to the grassy quad far below. I shook my head — that was too far to jump! He gestured again, and we stood on the sill. He opened his umbrella and held my hand. We jumped together, and the umbrella let us land softly. That was one of several "no way back, only forward" dreams I had during that time.

I hesitate to talk about dreams much, because, after several years of teaching the dream interpretation I'd learned, my dream-maker went on strike. In my dreams, I was only ever reading the plot of the dream in a book or a newspaper. I would read what happened, but there was no color, no movement, no smells or sounds. I stopped teaching about dreams, and slowly my own dreams came back, first as if I were hearing them through a wall, going on in the next room, then finally being able to inhabit them again.

I'm not superstitious about dreams, but they strike me as a good tool to use, an element, a story, or an image to help my thinking. So often, in problem solving, I can have a failure of imagination about my options. I think of the Tarot this way too, as John Sandford's character Kidd thinks of it in the context of game theory, an image or a thought to knock your thinking off dead center, to help you see all of your options, or to ask yourself better questions.

Looking back on the Pegasus dream, I see its truth. I've lived my life counting on the Muses, on their inspiration. I've always loved being in and near water. I don't know if Poseidon only rules the sea, or if he's involved in creeks, streams, and swimming pools. More research must be done. As far as my horse's mama, I have made a living helping people look at the fearsome Medusa-like things they are unable or unwilling to face alone. Poseidon, Medusa and the Muses, embodied in the strong winged horse carrying me. Feeling both safe and free is a rare and wonderful combination. People are so often willing to give up one for the other, and I'm full of gratitude for the flight I'm on, where I often get to feel both at the same time.

That summer was thirty-five years ago. Polly and Riggi are gone now. I carry both of them vividly in my mind. The things she taught me have stayed with me and helped me over and over. Riggi taught me too, that when someone is upset, just getting up and going to sit by them can help enormously.

Group

꙼

It's not a rule of friendship that you can only have one at a time. The kindergarten girl in the candy-striped glasses was mistaken. I wonder how many of the "rules for life" I hold in my mind and body came from other five- and six-year-olds? I never questioned the rule that girls can only marry boys and boys can only marry girls. That was the law of the land until a few years ago, so I will forgive myself for not thinking that far outside the box. For lesbians, it's also not a rule that all your friends have to be gay, and that if you love some straight women with your whole heart, it's not a rule that you want to be their girlfriend.

Here are some of the rules of friendship I've learned since kindergarten. It is good to spend quantity time as well as quality time with friends. It's important to hang out, talk about nothing and everything, and take walks if you can. There are three women in my chosen family who I talk to regularly. I don't live near them now, which is a sorrow for all of us. We try to talk often enough that our conversation isn't taken up with "and how's your husband? How are the grandchildren"? questions exclusively. We can take off from a minimal "everybody's fine" and go into politics or movies or work struggles or hair and clothing advice. Whatever direction we'd like to go. The friendship with two of them started when I was in my twenties. An older woman involved with my work told me I really should get to know Sudie, as she was also new to town and we would like each other. "Humph," I thought. I hadn't found that to work out well thus far. Sudie and I did have lunch, and we liked each other, surprisingly. She told me about a regular lunch she had with some other "Episcopalian ladies," and one of them was on staff at the Episcopal Church. Having watercress sandwiches with church ladies sounded like pure-t hell to me, so I gave a non-committal smile and told her I'd be glad to have lunch with just her again. She finally dragged me to the ladies lunch, where I found Sudie and two more women I liked a lot. We laughed at how I'd pictured them from Sudie's description.

"I thought, being a minister, that you would like the fact that they were both church people!" she said. It's complicated, I answered. The composition of the group changed over the years, but for fifteen years or so we met every Monday for lunch. We called it "Group." Some amazing women passed through that lunch gathering. It's down to three of us now, Sudie, Kate and me. We still meet online once a month or so. Group has been a gem in the middle of my life for more than thirty years now. They are my consulting committee, my kitchen cabinet. Once in a while we've gone on trips together. Up in the Blue Ridge Mountains, in Sudie's family's house in Blowing Rock, we walked around the hills collecting bittersweet vines for their bright orange berries. Decorating the mantelpieces with the bittersweet, we helped with the traditional rearranging of family photos to put the photos of Sudie's family in front and shuttled the other siblings' photos to the rear. We talked about what kind of dinner we might like. I said I'd always fantasized about an all-cheese dinner, with each course being a different cheese. They said I should have that. In the store we each picked out exactly what we would like to eat. We bought wine and brought everything back to the house. It was a lovely time of deep talking and mutual care. They talked me into staying with my husband, who I wanted to leave. This was before I had my sons. A dream I had up there led to that conversation over breakfast. I didn't leave the marriage, and I'm glad I stayed because my sons are the best people ever, and I'm glad to be their mom.

The third friend, Lola, I met when she wrote me a fan letter asking for hard copies of my radio commentaries for her mom in Georgia. We had lunch when I handed her the box of manuscripts, and hit it off splendidly. She's a veterinarian, and talks to me about mammalian behavior, among other things, of course. That information has come in handy in church work. I still send her my writings so she can tell me what she thinks, and we talk often.

Having friends who have known you forever is crucial; friends who have been with you through the end of your marriage, the shifting of your sexuality, and through all the other chances and changes of life. It's not good for a person to have to rely only on their own solitary brain for navigation through life. We need poetry, songs, Scriptures, therapists, family, coworkers, and friends. I think the rules for strengthening my relationship with all of those is the same — time spent. The same applies to my remarkable wife, the only person with whom I would joyfully embark on a six-week road trip.

Around the World with the Moonies

ॐ

One summer while I was at Converse, also before I had children, my Aunt Ruth invited me to apply to be part of a tour she was helping to lead. 130 men and women in our 20s would travel around the world, a two month trip, studying Christianity, Hinduism, Judaism, Taoism, Buddhism, Islam and Unificationism. The Moonies were paying. Other faculty members joked with me nervously that I might end up in airports selling flowers, which is what Moonie members did back then. That was before they bought fisheries in Massachusetts, *The Washington Times*, and other income generating properties.

Aunt Ruth and I had a blast in the crowd of people from all over the world. My roommate was from Sri Lanka, Tamil, living in India because of the war. She was funny and smart and had a wickedly elegant accent in which she could curse like a sailor. I hung out with Mormons, who were questioning their faith by the middle of the trip, with Sikhs, with a young man from a village in Burundi who would nearly weep as we gathered around the buffet at five-star hotels, beautiful ice sculptures gently dripping. "This would feed my whole village for a week," he would whisper.

We gathered into friend-clusters, went drinking in every country, laughed at the photos in each other's wallets, watched budding romances with great interest, sang together and learned about religion. In China we got to float in a red boat around a lily-studded lake with Houston Smith and his wife, which was like having an audience with the Pope. Which we also had, along with 12,000 other people in Saint Peter's Square. One of the young Jews on the trip was super excited because he got to touch the Pope's hand. He didn't wash that hand for days.

When I got home, it was time to start a family.

Sons

When my first son was born, I didn't know whether I could keep working full time. As it turned out, I couldn't. After my maternity leave was over, I put him in a home day care, and I had to go visit him a couple of times a week during the day because I missed him so much. I'd been working on certification as a pastoral counselor, and I got a job at the Methodist counseling center up the road from the college. That job was part time, and it gave me a lot more time with the baby.

Working as a counselor was satisfying. My mentor, Mitch, was a kind, patient and persistent teacher. Trained by him and a few others, I eventually reached the Fellow level in the American Association of Pastoral Counselors, where I could supervise other counselors. After a few years I opened my own office on the main square of the town. I had my name painted in gold on the second story window, and it looked so much like the detective agency in a noir film that it made me happy to look at it. I heard so many stories in that office: moving, terrible, hilarious, awful and amazing stories. I watched people work with me to get better, and I watched people work against me and themselves to stay the way they were. I heard so much pain. I tried to leave it at the office so it wouldn't affect my family. I don't know that I was successful in that effort.

After a couple of years we had another baby, and I was a very happy mama. I never knew if I was a good mother. There is always a sneaking suspicion that you're not doing it right, and I definitely didn't know what I was doing. I loved being pregnant. I'd always been overweight, but now I didn't care. This round belly had something wonderful in it. That something wonderful was a beloved and demanding being. When it was time for a nap, it was as if my passenger had pulled the emergency brake on the train. Screeching to a halt, I would lie down on the floor of my office and sleep. Hunger was the same way. Hungry. NOW. That didn't change much after the wonderful being was born. I marveled at how self-centered babies are. No one had talked about that. How the baby wants to breastfeed every hour and a half for twenty minutes, until your nipples are cracked and bleeding, until you are psychotic from lack of sleep. People do talk about the love, but they can't describe it: the instant ferocity of the love I felt for my sons, that I would paint myself blue and run screaming into battle for them, and that I would spend hours staring into their beautiful faces. There were difficult moments, but I remember it as all joy.

Sam, our firstborn, could not understand why we thought we needed another child. He was mad all the time, stormy mad. One night when he was five I asked him about it. "Why are you so mad all the time"?

"I have been mad since Ned was born," he said.

"What do you think we can do about that"? I asked. "What could make it better"?

"Well," he said thoughtfully, "you could buy me more toys."

My mother was a loving and laissez-faire parent in some ways. In India, she said, children were allowed to run wild until they were about five. I have no idea whether that was or is true. She said I had good instincts, and I should just follow my instincts rather than reading a bunch of books about children. She died seven years before my first child was born, but I remembered what she said, and carried that baby everywhere with me. He was gorgeous fun, except when he woke up, as I've told you, to nurse every hour and a half all night, when I began to wonder whether he was a Demon Seed.

As a mom, I guess I mostly copied my parents. They were good enough parents. They tried to teach me their values; they tried to keep me safe insofar as it was within their powers. My father was tenderhearted. He'd been spanked a lot as a kid, and he vowed never to spank my sister or me. I spanked my sons a couple of times, but they would say "didn't hurt," and laugh, and I would laugh too, frustrated, embarrassed, and completely unwilling to do it so that it did hurt. Instead of spanking, my dad would sit me down and talk to me about his disappointment, about the reasons for the rule, and ask about why I'd done a thing. It worked. My mother wasn't averse to spanking, but the way she did it wasn't humiliating or even that noticeable. I remember her doing it once in a while, but it felt like a quick course correction rather than any deeply involved kind of punishment.

I was sure I didn't want to teach them the religion of my childhood. Their dad was a Presbyterian minister, as I had been, so they got some regular mainline Protestant teaching at his church. I taught them my beliefs, which were that everything is interconnected, that you should be kind and love yourself, one another, and the planet. Mama tried to teach us her strict Scottish Presbyterian religion, but at the same time, she taught us its loopholes. You already know she let us play "Battleship" on Sabbath if we called it "Going to Jerusalem."

Mama was fun. She'd worked as a camp counselor all the summers of her late teens, so she knew how to hike and sail. She loved to ride her bike and take us camping. We had a cream-colored VW camper with a pop up top. We'd picked it up one summer in Germany, named it Vernon, drove all over the place, and shipped it back to the states in September. She drove happily, not necessarily planning where we would go next or which camp site we'd use. We drove until she was ready to stop, and we'd find ourselves a campground. In Europe, most of the campgrounds were just big open fields, and she'd putter around until she saw a pup tent with a space next to it. Pup tents meant teen boys, and she knew that meant happy teenage girls. She'd park, we'd set up the tent, she'd put on a pot of spaghetti and go knock on the pup tent. Often the boys would emerge. She'd ask them if she could string a clothesline from our van to their tent, and by the way would they like to come to supper? We'd build a fire and play guitar. We'd go out every summer, for six weeks at a time, to Europe, Scandinavia, the Western US, anywhere she had a hankering to see. We would alternate years, my sister and I, being able to invite a friend. Once we invited a fun cousin to go with us to California. We all got baptized by the Calvary Chapel people in the Pacific Ocean. I remember being knee deep in the waves, in a crush of young people, and my cousin muttering darkly, "I'm not sure I want to be cleansed of ALL my sins…"

For a trip to the White Mountains, I invited a boy I liked. Mama let us sleep in the tent together after a brief test of wills. "Avoid the appearance of evil," she said.

"Ma, he's gay," I said. He wasn't.

I never did take my boys hiking or camping. We didn't make kites or build boats in the garage and sail them to the islands. They played outside, I let them climb, figuring that, if they broke something it could mostly be fixed, and that what would be hard to fix would be if I instilled fear or timidity in them. When they came inside with their friends I would make Earl Grey tea, which they all loved, because I added plenty of sugar. Yes, I was a pusher for Earl Grey, getting all the neighborhood boys hooked.

I did end up reading a couple of books that helped with parenting. One was by an Adlerian psychologist called *Children, the Challenge*, and it talked about how not to get in power struggles with children. Give them choices, it said. "Time for bed! Do you want to wear the yellow PJs or the blue ones"? In an emotionally neutral tone: "Do you want to behave better and stay here in the restaurant or do you want to go sit in the car with me"? Giving people a choice is a good strategy in lots of situations. "You may either stop messing up my church and stay or you may continue that behavior and go somewhere else." The Montessori School they went to used that technique as well, so in situations with difficult adults we've started saying "Time to Montessori their ass." The other book was a dog-training manual by the Monks of New Skete. From them I learned to "catch" them doing something good and praise that instead of catching them doing something bad and giving that a lot of energy. They said the point of training your dog is to invite them to be a good companion to you and to be useful in the world. That sounded like a good plan for training human mammals as well.

To prepare them for the world, I thought about how our culture punishes bad behavior. You either get a fine or get a time out in prison. (Ideally. I know that's not how things actually work much of the time.) So they would get a bag of nickels, then, as they grew older, quarters, at the beginning of the week. Whatever they had left over they could keep. When they bickered, I'd warn them and then fine them a quarter. Likewise for other annoying behavior. Sometimes they'd get a time out. Sometimes a toy or a game that was causing problems would get a time out, living on top of the fridge for a while. I don't know. Things that work on one kid won't work on another one. Parenting is not for the faint of heart.

What did I learn about parenting from my dad, besides having an aversion to spanking? That is a more complicated answer. Can a parent love a child too much? I was too important to him. Whenever he was home, my sister would be allowed to go hang out with Mama in the kitchen, or even go up to her room alone. I had to be in the same room with him, engaged with him, playing chess or doing math homework. He loved explaining math. He was like James Michener, going all the way back to the bedrock to explain the process of a problem. I felt overwhelmed and impatient most of the time, but I was grateful during the SAT where I'd forgotten how to do simple long division but I was able to go back to the bedrock and figure it out.

He talked to me about inappropriate things, the details of the world's suffering that came across the AP wire into the CBS newsroom where he worked, sexual things people did that I hadn't yet imagined or thought about, his own depression. The times he'd considered suicide were not what I needed to hear about when I was a child. I worried all the time about whether he was going to stay alive, and how I could be enough to keep him alive. I have no idea whether he thought about the effects such confessions would have on me, how much too heavy they were for my spirit. I heard about his thoughts on marrying my mother. "I didn't want my life anymore, and she did, so I gave it to her." I heard about his long time love, Carol, who he'd loved at first sight when he was seventeen, right after his mother had died. She was his secretary for years, and the love of his life, I think. If they'd divorced their spouses and married each other, that would have been one thing. She kept trying to let me get to know her, but she was stupid about it. The first stupidity was that I could see she was trying to horn in on my mother, which made me hate her. Aside even from that she wasn't a nice person. I think she was what they would have called in the "Mad Men" days, "a man's woman." She tried to talk to me about how pretty she was, for god's sake. Who would think that was a good idea?

I heard and saw too much for a kid, but it wasn't as bad as what many other kids hear and see every day. Still, down that road lies the minimization and dismissal of pain endemic to my culture, so I'm going to just go ahead and say it sucked. As I've said before, I had the whole entire "Chosen Child" syndrome where you feel proud and almost superhuman because one of your parents has given you a role in their lives much more suited to another adult, and at the same time you feel an ongoing inadequacy because there is no way for a child to do a good job being an adult companion to their parent.

I learned not to lean on my sons for friendship or partnership. That feels important. I love them, give advice when asked (mostly) and trust them to be themselves. I learned to let my religion be an undercurrent, rather than something that snaked through every interaction, every sentence. The way the Bible was pushed on me as a child feels invasive. It was there, weighing heavily on top of every conversation, intruding, consent or no consent. My sons got to avoid that. I wish I'd cooked for them better when they were living with me, but I didn't. Eating intelligently was something they've had to learn as adults, but they have figured that out and more, making up for my failings as a mom and their father's failings as a dad. I don't know how to make up for my father's failings as a grandfather. My older son was twenty years old the first time my dad asked how they were doing.

Warmth, Light, Fire

॰ঃ

The sprout from a broken-open seed seeks the sun. A good bit of the warmth and light my spirit found was with the Unitarian Universalists. The first time the tiny UU congregation in town had asked me to come speak, I was the Presbyterian college chaplain at the nearby women's college. "Don't preach a Presbyterian sermon," Margaret, my contact, said. "Do some research on UU and preach a UU kind of sermon." I arrived early at the little blue house on a side street near the college where they met. There was room for two cars in the driveway. While the service was getting set up, I cracked open a hymnal and began to read. The songs were familiar, but the words were better. In the way back of the book were readings. Rabindranath Tagore, T.S. Eliot, Adrienne Rich! Marge Piercy! My heart began to wake up. During the service there was a time for spoken joys and concerns. A deep voiced woman stood up at her seat and said "I saw a pileated woodpecker in my back yard this week," then she sat down. Nothing about The Lord or The Creation, just joy in a woodpecker. The feeling of freedom, being able to talk about what was in my mind and heart, was exhilarating. I had found my people! They asked me back several times over the next few years, and I started to explore ways of transferring my ordination from Presbyterian to UU.

One of the women in Group was a member of that congregation. She came in one day for lunch and slapped some papers down on the table. "Here. This is your kind of thing." I looked at the descriptions of a women's spirituality retreat: mountain air, workshops on drumming and massage, Tarot, painting and mask making. The other two regulars looked it over too.

"We want you to go," the Unitarian said, and the Methodist and the Episcopalian nodded gamely. "We're going too, so you don't have to go by yourself the first time." The first night of the retreat, I shimmered with the elation of seeing there could be such joy, joy like in a Pentecostal service, but without the bad theology. I was dancing, whirling, grinning, and they were sedately leaning against the wall, arms folded, watching me with great affection. That's how you do it. That's how you introduce someone to a piece of your religion that you know they need. She companioned me right into the faith that now grounds and nourishes me.

Navigating by New Stars

༄

For a long time I tried to let the witchiness and the Christianity exist side by side. My Aunt Ruth, after all, was an Episcopal priest. It was my sexuality sliding to the gay side that finally just tore it up.

I'd made good friends at the women's spirituality gatherings. It was intoxicating for a married mom of two sons who spent most of her time in boy-world to come to girl world for a visit. Late one night, around eleven, I dropped in on the dance in the rec hall. One of my dear friends was dancing there. We looked enough alike back then so that people got us mixed up all the time. They would come to me to finish a conversation they'd started with her. We danced for a minute, me dancing with this woman I loved, with myself, and something hit me like a train. I was in love with this person. I turned and ran. Climbing the fire tower to get up into the mountain air, to see things from some distance, I found a group of women up there. I stood at the railing of the tower, feeling the wind coming up the mountain. It started to feel like it was coming just for me. I raised my arms and let it blow through me. Whatever happened between my friend and me, I know things had changed in a big way. I lay down with my head in the center of a star-shape of women, our heads together on the high wooden platform. We stared at the stars, which were close and bright. One by one, we began renaming all of the constellations, names that had meaning for our lives. It was going to be all new navigation from here on out.

The witchiness and the Christianity had existed side by side for a time, but once this new thing bloomed, it was time to make big changes.

I couldn't see a way to stay in the marriage to this Presbyterian minister who couldn't say *I love you* or *good morning*, who would have been happiest as a Jesuit who could read and teach and spend a lot of time alone. And watch sports on TV. Basketball, Golf, Football, we watched them all. Again I was overwhelmed by the feeling of being in an ill-fitting life. I loved my counseling work, although I was burning out quickly, I loved my round garden, and I adored being a mother to my sons, but the rest of it felt wrong.

Interim

ॐ

I didn't know what to do until the President of the Board of the local UU congregation reached out to me to ask if I would consider being their Interim Minister. Yes, I would, if it could last two years. It could, he said. It was time I could use to change my ordination to UU, to get my children settled in this new family arrangement where their mom and dad lived separately, and while I saw what would be left of my counseling practice.

I told the church trustees I was getting a divorce, and they accepted going with me through whatever turmoil might come with that. I'd been one of the main couples counselors in town, but as my marriage ended, my energy for that work was gone. I knew I was burned out when I found myself talking too much, too full of opinions about what my clients should do. The day I knew I needed to quit was when I leaned forward and told a long-time client "Please do. Not. Marry. That. Man." She did, of course, and they had a lovely child. Then they divorced and she married the one she should have married in the first place. I hope they are living happily ever after.

As soon as word of my divorce made its way around the place, the main people who came to counseling were people who wanted permission to get a divorce too.

Leaving

༄

There is no way to leave someone that will make them say "Good job, you left me as well as you could."

Ending a marriage is a terrible job. After my Christianity fell apart and I found work where I could put my heart, after I fell in love with my best friend, I knew that I needed to be in the church where my spirit could blossom, and I knew I needed to be with a woman partner. I tried to figure out how to do this and stay married. That was sad and stupid. Hurtful all around.

All my life I'd pictured myself with my finger on a thread that was guiding me. *The Princess and the Goblin* had been a favorite book when I was a girl, and there is a scene in it (I think it's in that one) where the Princess finds herself in a cave, unable to tell in the dark which way to turn. She reaches out her hand and finds a thread strung there, and if she runs her finger along the thread she can go where it goes and be guided. I'd had my thread my whole life, and, after fourteen years of marriage, it took a hard turn toward leaving. This is not a decision I wanted to make. I had two young sons, and they didn't need to go through that pain. I stood stock still for three years, unwilling to move on without my thread, unwilling to follow it out of the marriage. I prayed, in my way, speaking with my spirit guides.

"We don't care anything about marriage," they said. "It is a made-up thing. We care about love. Are you loving? Are you being loved? Are you following your thread"? Finally I did it.

My husband was hurt and angry. "You're killing me. You are killing your children," he said. For many years the anger grew. The phone calls were so awful I wrote him that he had lost his privilege of talking to me on the phone, and he'd have to do it by email from then on. The emails were so awful I finally asked a friend at work to read them for me and just tell me the information I needed: when to meet him so he could be with the boys, when and where to pick them up. When I finally said to him "the person who reads your emails for me says you want to pick up at this time, but I wonder if we could do this other time," the nasty emails stopped. Divorce was awful and crazy-making for us, but I have never thought I shouldn't have done it. It hurt my sons, and for that I am deeply sorry. I don't know what else I could have done.

In the small Southern town where we lived, as I've said, I lost my juice for couples counseling. Grateful for the Interim job at the UU church, I rented a house in the most respectable old-money neighborhood in town, right behind the school where all the white Junior League mommies took their kids. People are like chickens, and I knew that if I ducked my head in shame even a little bit I would be pecked to death.

Things with the friend I'd fallen in love with didn't work out, because she was straight. After a while, I fell in love with a woman who had two foster-daughters, and who lived in a small mountain town an hour and a half's drive away. It was just right for me, still mightily jumpy about commitment of any kind. The four of us, two white moms, two milk-colored kids, one coffee colored kid and one caramel colored kid, aroused curiosity wherever we went. The general public were polite, and the Unitarians were thrilled, as we increased the diversity of their congregation. Yes, some friends with a lot to lose dropped me. Folks moved over so they wouldn't be seen sitting next to me at my sons' church league basketball games. The surprising person who sat right with me and actually talked to me was Eunice, the mother of the woman my ex-husband had married. "I just think people should act like a family," she said. God bless her forever. That kind of public help makes all the difference.

As I said, even with my head held high, I'd have been pecked to death in the small Southern town if my best friend hadn't been Sudie, one of the most popular and richest women in town, married to a home town boy made good. Under her aegis, I was untouchable in a way that could never otherwise have happened. She could have abandoned me when it became generally known that I'd "turned gay." People in that southern town couldn't decide which was worse, turning gay or leaving Christianity for the Unitarians. You can be "a little funny" sexually in most Southern towns, and many people are, but when you stop believing that Jesus is the son of God and the savior of humankind, you've gone over the line. Some people still spoke to me, but a few pointedly turned their backs on me at the grocery store. My beautiful friend stayed with me through all of that. God bless her forever too. My fall from the town's grace was eased by these kind people. I can't think how hard it would have been without them.

I lived in that town for ten more years, reared my sons there, and I hold that congregation in my heart. They hired me as their Interim while I was still married, but they knew a divorce was coming. Several months later at a board meeting, I asked them to go into Executive Session, which means no notes will be taken for the public minutes.

"I've come to the realization that in order to live my life with authenticity, to blossom in a new way, I need to live it as an out lesbian." There was much nodding, reassuring smiles.

One gay man at the end of the table said "Just don't think that this is going to be good news for everyone. I mean, tell anyone you want but don't expect them to be happy for you." The voice of experience, I knew. I nodded.

The secretary asked "Well, what should I write in the notes"?

The man who recruited me, a professor with great gravitas, said "Just write that we went into Executive Session —- and then we came out!"

The Church

᠅

Church work is the family business. On my
mother's side of the family there has been a minister
in the family in every generation since 1690. They
were southern preachers with sonorous voices, good
story tellers, funny, self-deprecating, well respected.
On my father's side, his dad was the first, but he
made quite a splash. Preaching in a big Presbyterian
church in Philadelphia, founding *Eternity* magazine
and the *Bible Study Hour*, heard far and wide on the
radio, traveling the world to preach to big crowds,
he was a famous face, a famous voice, a famous
name. A Big Man.

Most of the southern family, my mother's
family, were dubious about my being a minister. I
remember one Thanksgiving family reunion when
we all gathered outside my Uncle Shem's house for
a photograph. That was going to be a good time for
the before-dinner blessing, so Shem called out from
his ladder where he'd been perched for the
photograph, "Who is the minister here today"? My
cousin, standing behind me in the crowd of sixty or
so people, said my name. Shem just went on,
though, answering his own question. One of the
second or third cousins had just graduated from
seminary, or maybe he was still a student. Shem
called out his name, proudly announcing that this
young man could say the blessing. A couple of

people slid their eyes toward me, seeing how I would react, maybe? With apology, maybe? I bit the insides of my cheeks, having been in ministry several years by that time, determined not to cry in front of these people.

Some years later, at another reunion, my cousin Rebecca, the host, asked me to say the blessing. I did, and a couple of people sidled up to me to say under their breath, "good job." The polite southern thing to do when someone behaves outlandishly is to ignore them, smile past them, let your eyes slide over them. That's how most of them handled my being a minster.

I came to church work late in my ministry. For years I worked as a chaplain, then as a pastoral counselor. Becoming a Unitarian Universalist enabled me to work in churches. The work suits me well. In churches I see all of the stages of the lives of the "seeds" who are planted all around me. There is room for close attention, for the big picture as well as the small picture. It feels like being a gardener.

Singing and What It Led To

Walking down the sidewalk with the family, my dad would burst into song. He had an operatic baritone, and whatever he sang sounded beautiful. It was a little embarrassing, though, on the street. His sister was a professional mezzo-soprano. I think everyone in the family could sing a little.

The family sang together from time to time. I didn't like it because I was the tenor voice, and singing that low made me yawn. Maybe I should've breathed more? I learned to read music doing this. I always had a piano teacher of one kind or another, but they always grew frustrated because I had perfect big hands for the piano but I wouldn't practice.

When I was twelve I asked for a guitar. My father and I went to the music store and for some reason came home with a twelve-string guitar. "Do you know how to tune it"? Daddy asked me in the store. I admitted I didn't. "Well," he said, a little grumpy and bemused, "you've got a lot of nerve getting this guitar when you don't even know how to tune it." I didn't know what to say to that. The helpful fellow at the store showed me how to tune it. I had a guitar teacher for a minute, as I've told you, which was helpful for a start, but he wanted me to learn kids' songs. I bought a Joan Baez song book and learned every song. I think I wrote one during that time, but I don't remember it at all. I played a lot in college. In the freshman dorm I heard a plaintiff high-lonesome song coming from a room with an open door. I stood there to listen and met Julia from Asheville. We sang Appalachian sex-and-death songs together and became good friends. "Ten years ago on a cold, dark night, someone was killed 'neath the town hall light. The people who saw, they all agreed that the slayer who ran looked a lot like me."

We branched out into God songs, because in Appalachia you've got sex, death, and God. And you've got rich white people coming in to swindle you out of your land, dirtying or diverting your water, and taking the tops off of the mountains. There are plenty of songs about that too. "Daddy, won't you take me back to Muhlenberg County, down by the Green River where Paradise lay. I'm sorry my son, but you're too late in asking, Mr. Peabody's coal train done hauled it away." Singing with another person lights up your brain. I saw it in Bobby McFerrin's documentary *Music Instinct: Science and Song*. Someone in a scanner sang alone, then sang with his bandmate, and whole different areas of his brain lit up on the monitor. We liked the way it felt.

After I fell in with the Christians and joined JC Power and Light Company. I played rhythm guitar and sang too high. We toured on Spring Break, all over the Southeast. Soon a rock band emerged from the folk group, and I was invited to be in that. "The Damascus Road Experience," they called it. I joked that Paul was blinded on the Damascus Road, and we were more likely to deafen you. Those boys liked to play loudly. One of them, a passionate stocky young man with longish black hair noticed that I sang a lot better when I sang in a lower register. I tried it. It reminded me of singing tenor in the family group, so I was resistant, but he was right. I could belt it out if I sang lower.

It wasn't until *Radio Free Bubba* that I started singing regularly to people. Pat Jobe had invited me into the *Bubba* rotation, and Hub City publishers in Spartanburg had published our book, *The Best of Radio Free Bubba*. We started a book tour. Barnes & Noble in Greenville was an awful experience. It wasn't their fault; it followed the pattern of most book signings. They set the authors up at a table near the front and we sat there. People coming into the store saw us, and gave us a wide berth so they didn't have to interact. It was embarrassing and a little bit lonely, although the three of us loved each other and had a good time just hanging out. At our second stop on the tour, Pat told me he was going to bring his guitar just to keep us entertained. I said I'd bring mine too, so we sat at the Table of Isolation and Shame and played songs for each other. People began to come over to listen. We sold some books. We brought our guitars every time after that, and it became part of our book tour. We started writing funny songs together. "Born codependent way down in Cumming, Georgia, so sad to hurt my mama on a Saturday night." I wrote "The A.D.D. Blues" and "The Bipolar Waltz." Three out of four of my bipolar friends said the song was fine, but I got some outraged pushback from folks who weren't ready to see the lighter side of it, so I don't sing it any more. I don't want to hurt anybody. Maybe I was born codependent too, like the woman we wrote the song about.

The Interim ministry at the Spartanburg church was over, but my counseling practice wasn't building back up to where it had been. I had some savings because Mark had bought me out of the house, but they were going, going, gone. I had to stay in town because the boys were half the time with me and half with Mark, and I didn't want to take them away from their dad. I was about to take a job counseling children who had been abused. I knew that job would kill me. I prayed hard, which included doing some magic.

I Did Some Magic

One time I said something too lightly and there was, in it, a disrespect. Someone had asked whether people could get fixated on using magic as a quick fix to their problems. "If only magic worked as a quick fix," I said. "Usually, though, you can bibbity-bobbity-boo all over your problems and you look up and they're still there. Who's going to get fixated on that"? I should have gone on to say "Deep magic, though, deep magic demands effort and change." I wish I'd said something more respectful like that, but I'm used to keeping silent about my feelings about magic. This is where I do a little coming out.

Things work mysteriously in my life. My rational side doesn't believe in praying to saints, but when I lose something I say "St. Anthony, St. Anthony, please come around. My phone is lost and it must be found." A lot of times, I'll get a mind-picture of where something is, or I look one more time in a place I looked twice before and there it is. I don't believe in this, but sometimes it works. I believe in the laws of thermodynamics too, but sometimes I look in the same drawer three times and the lost thing isn't there. The fourth time, there it is, easily visible. At our house, we call that "gremlins." As I was writing this, I lost my debit card. Looking through the hotel room, shaking out all my clothes, searching my pocketbook over and over, it was nowhere. I felt that I knew the restaurant where I'd left it, but the place was closed for holidays. The bank would give me another, but it was also closed for holidays. I resigned myself to using a credit card until the banks opened again, but then I realized I hadn't talked to St. Anthony. "St Anthony, St. Anthony, please come around, my debit card is lost and it must be found." Three minutes later I was putting on my shoes. When I put my left foot down, it slid, as if something slick were on the floor. Lifting my foot, there was the debit card, under my shoe, where it hadn't been (I would swear) when I picked up the shoe to put it on.

I don't believe in hands-on healing, either, but I have been helped by Reiki and I've helped others by doing it for them. My rational mind understands that I really want magic to be true. I don't believe in supernatural magic that breaks whatever laws there are in the universe (even though they seem to break themselves once in a while). I want it to exist in the world, not in some kind of supernatural way, but in a way that is consonant with the natural world, part of it that we haven't figured out yet how to detect or measure. So many people experience these mysterious confluences that it would be unscientific to ignore them. They remain unexplained, and yet there they are.

When I did magic that night for an after-Interim job, it worked! I wrote down what I wanted in a job. Enough money to take care of my children and myself. Part time, so I could be with them after school. I wanted to like the people I worked with and I asked to laugh every day. Rolling up the paper with my list on it, and trying with a string, I put in on my altar and lit a candle. "I'm not the person for this job with these children," I said out loud. "It will kill me."

A voice said back to me (not out loud, just as if I were remembering a conversation in my mind) "Would you work in a factory"?

"Yes," I answered unequivocally. "I'll do whatever."

I lit a candle and let it burn until I went to bed. In the morning I got a phone call from my friend Pat Jobe, a co-author on our book *Best of Radio Free Bubba*.

"Margaret Ann," he said, "can you drive a tow motor"?

"Pat, I don't know what a tow motor is, but I can learn."

"There's a job here at Charlie's place. You get to go to the bathroom twice a day and you get half an hour for lunch. Want to come interview"?

"Shall I wear my new silk interview suit"?

"Well, you can bring it if you want," he said, and I heard Charlie laughing in the background. Charlie had liked my stories when he'd come to the *Bubba* book tour shows, especially the one where I'd quoted Butch Hancock: "Life in Lubbock, Texas, taught me two things: One is that God loves you and you're going to burn in hell. The other is that sex is the most awful, filthy thing on earth and you should save it for someone you love." That had made Charlie guffaw. Thanks, Butch.

Pat and I kept our guitars by our desks, wrote songs, played our songs for each other, talked to Charlie about life, love, God, sex and everything else. I cold-called useful men who knew how to make things and fix things. I hadn't known that kind of man before. The men in my life had been scholars and clergy, performers and clinicians. Industry men were a refreshing change, as was calling people who didn't want to talk to me. That is the opposite of parish ministry, and it was restful. We laughed out loud every day because Pat and Charlie are the funniest people I've ever known. I made enough money to live and I got to sped afternoons with my boys.

The magic worked, but it demanded that I let go of thinking of myself as solely a minister and therapist — just for a few years. Working Charlie's job moved a stiff-necked self-definition and made room for more humility, creativity, friendship, awareness, and fun. I didn't "bibbity-bobbity boo" over my financial panic, but I surrendered, willing for deep magic to work, and its gifts were profound. I don't turn to it often, though, wary of its demands.

I don't think that magic is anything supernatural. I think it's part of the natural world that moves in us and through us. A lot of flakes and sinners use it to bamboozle the needy and gullible, but they use faith, love and hope that way too, and I wouldn't be willing to scorn those because they are hard to measure and sometimes get used for dishonorable purposes. I'll keep being open to the deep magic, and practicing it, until I find a way to believe in it.

All Will Be Well

೩೯

I kept singing, with Pat and without him. The UU congregation where I'd been Interim had settled a minister, and then when he left, had another Interim. They did a national search for a new minister, and I applied, having been separated from them for the requisite number of years. They called me to serve them as their settled (permanent) minister, and a new chapter began. I sang to that congregation. I wrote them songs for special occasions. We had a jam night every week, and I'd bring my new non-church songs there. I began singing the benediction at the end of the services.

"All Will Be Well" started coming to me while I was driving. My sons were small, and I'd dropped them off at school. "Do you not know. Do you not know" started repeating in my mind. I'd written a piece about Julian of Norwich and her famous saying "All will be well, and all will be well, and all manner of things will be well." I'd decided it was a good mantra for me, even if I didn't understand it. Things were so plainly not well everywhere. Evildoers and self-righteous people were making hell for others in the name of their own pleasure or their twisted beliefs. Eventually I came to believe that the energy of love remains in the "air" forever, while everything else fades. That's what I decided, or that's how I was guided. Only love lasts. Not romantic love, but the energy from acts of love between humans, animals, and other beings who are helpful and kind add to the river of love in the world. More about this later. So eventually all will be well. I hear from people pretty often about the part that song has played in their lives, and I'm grateful every time. People like others among my songs, but that's the one I hear about most. I feel I've been of use in the world, having written that one and sung it to so many people. Kiya, who is a classically trained musician and composer, wrote an arrangement of it so now choirs are singing it too, and that is a joy to know.

When I was injured for such a long time some years ago, people kept saying it back to me. From the depths of pain and the daily fight against despair, the words were not a comfort. All will be well, yeah, except I may not ever walk easily again. All will be well, yeah, and I'll be getting used to using scooters and wheel chairs. All will be well, but maybe this song is all about death. All will be well at my death. Is that what it means? Sitting in an orthopedic recliner for seven months, recovering from one hip replacement after the other on the same hip every six weeks, just getting to where I could walk a little, then going back under the knife, forbidden from putting any weight on that side for six more weeks, hopping along on a walker or crutching along, I moved painfully. All will be well, but damn it hurts and I can't work and I'm burning my sabbatical being injured and I'm mad about all of it, especially at the voices (within me and outside me) wanting me to make meaning out of this while

I'm in the very goddam middle of it. One thing I like about the song is that the chorus goes to the minor at the end, as if to say this isn't a cheerleader song. I could be wrong about all of it. What I really mean to say is that song is an expression of my faith, and my faith was shaken during this period of being injured.

The Injury

ॐ

What happened? Always a horsey girl, I loved to ride. When my parents had money I had lessons, a proper black velvet helmet, and helpful staff at the stable. When I was fourteen the money was gone and my friend Lois and I rode at this place run by an old drunk named Howard. He liked to pretend we had dirt or a piece of hay stuck to our t-shirts, and he wanted to help brush it off. We ignored that because it was cheap there and he didn't make us wear helmets. I don't remember much about the horse I was riding the day I fell, except that he loved the barn. Lois and I were in the ring taking our horses over low jumps, and my horse caught sight of the barn and made the decision without me to jump the outer fence of the ring itself and head on up the hill to the barn. I fell off and hit hard. Lois said my eyes turned blue and then rolled up into my head. I'll buy that part about rolling up into my head. I had a concussion, and lost my memory for a few days. I don't remember being taken to the doctor. That may be part of the memory loss, though.

Five years later I was limping badly, and pains were shooting up and down my leg. Arthritis, the doctor said. "That's ridiculous," I thought. "I'm nineteen years old." By the time I was thirty and pregnant, it was nearly unbearable. The doctors in

Spartanburg told me to take more Advil. I was too young for a hip replacement. They wore out, they said, and would have to be rebuilt, and the rebuilds often didn't work out well. After Sam was born I went to the doctor at Duke. Hip replacements were fairly new, and they were doing them there. Dr. Nuneley took me on, and replaced the hip. I was sent home with the advice to do leg raises and walk a little. I was to be off the leg for two months to allow the bones to grown in around the prosthesis. My mother-in-law came to help take care of Sam, and we got through it with her help. I got my life back. I still limped, but I could walk wherever I wanted and I could do karate. That hip lasted thirty years.

"It's time to do a rebuild," the Austin doctor said. "The old prosthesis has come loose and it's chipping away at your pelvis. It's nearly broken through, and you won't like what happens if it breaks through. We're going to have to rebuild the pelvis with bone from the bone bank. You won't be able to put weight on this for six weeks." Everything went ok. Until three weeks after the surgery when I woke up in a cold sweat, shaking uncontrollably. Kiya tried to hold me and warm me, but it only ended up shaking her too. I took some Advil, and it calmed down a little.

We decided I should go on to the doctor to have him check everything out. They stuck a long needle into the joint and came out with bad news. Staph infection, I was going to need to have another surgery to take out part of the prosthesis, and we'd keep our fingers crossed that the infection was on those easy-to-remove parts. I started a three times a day infusion of killer antibiotics through a PICC line they inserted into my arm. It delivered the meds right next to my heart. The doctor who put in the PICC line said I could pick out any music I wanted while they put it in. I turned up Tribe Called Red and they got me through.

Seven o'clock AM, three o'clock PM, and eleven o'clock PM were the exact times to do the infusion. Once a week we had to go in to the infusion center where the nurse would clean the line. I had to turn my head so as not to breathe on it. Everything had to be as clean as possible. We would bring the empty Styrofoam medicine cooler and the pharmacist would fill it with new balls of antibiotics. They looked a little like plastic Christmas tree ornaments. You'd attach the ball, flip the little release lever and wait forty-five minutes while the ball emptied itself into your arm. We would imagine the meds as releasing hundreds of Star Wars x-wing fighters into my bloodstream. "Go, little x-wings!" we'd say.

In the second surgery, they took out the parts that could easily be removed and replaced them. In hopes that the infection was clinging to those pieces. Four weeks later the right side of my pants were wet with drainage, and the infusion doc looked at the incision and said it didn't look good. The infection was still active.

A third surgery was scheduled, and they took everything out, including the thirty-year-old rod that went down into my thigh bone. That was a violent procedure, where they had to break things to get it all out. They put in spacers covered in antibiotic ointment. Those never feel right, and they hurt. You can't really recover when you have spacers in. Six weeks later they went in again, took out the spacers, and put in a new prosthesis. After that, and after the ten weeks of antibiotics were over, the infection was finally gone. The only problem with this recovery was that they had damaged the femoral nerve, so my knee and thigh were like a numb sandbag. I couldn't flex my thigh muscle. My knee wouldn't hold, and collapsed in scary ways. Even now, years later, my foot is numb, my knee is unstable, and the muscles they cut through so many times are not doing their job. The muscles are unconscious, and only wake up now and then when the PT and I try really hard. I'm discouraged and angry. I want to walk, but I can't walk far. The muscles around the "unconscious" ones are trying to pitch in, but that's not what they are built for, so they fatigue quickly. I need to use a chair when we go to a museum or on a longer adventure. I use hiking poles, and they help some.

I don't know how to make meaning out of all of this, and I don't owe it to anyone to make meaning about it in any public way. I feel some solidarity from the folks in my congregation who use walkers, crutches and chairs. They watched me get better, and rooted for me with great compassion. I am still working on having compassion for myself.

I had a dream while I was in the chair that I was on the phone with my agent, a video call. We were talking about my fiction book, but my wife Kiya's band started to play and I couldn't hear her. I told her I was going outside so I could hear my agent better. Opening the front door, I was blocked by vines and lilacs. Their sweet bulk fell against me, and kept me from going out. I love the smell of lilacs, I love the feel of lilacs. I imagine this dream was saying that there was some sweetness in that trapped situation.

I'm convinced it changed me, but I'm not sure how. Not being able bodied is nothing new to me, but I'm still dealing with the emotional fallout. My father taught me to stride, long steps, covering ground fast. I could almost keep up with him. He didn't see the point in going up stairs one at a time. Vigor was a foundational principle for him, and he always took stairs two at a time. He was in a wheelchair almost all the time for the three years before he died. I can only imagine what that did to his spirit.

My wife is a walker. I can't walk with her. She wants to go on walking trips, on long pilgrimages. I want to go with her, and our plan is for me to write in a pub or a coffee shop while she does the day's miles, then meet her at the end point.

I Used To Be a Praying Kid

༄

Did I pray during this ordeal? It depends on what you mean by "pray." I used to be a praying kid. Lying in bed before sleep, I would pray for the people I loved, I would pick through my worries and lift them up so God could see, asking for help and guidance. Sometimes I would end with contemplating eternity. I would think "It goes forever, and ever, and ever, until…wait, there is no until. It goes forever, and ever, and ever…..zzzzz" I remember being excited one night about how long I thought I had prayed, and I got out of bed to tell my mother. I burst into the room where the grownups were talking and told them excitedly that I'd prayed for almost AN HOUR!" I still remember their amused looks, approving but puzzled. I had a flash of wondering whether I was the only person here taking this praying thing seriously. Then I was embarrassed, and wondered if it had really been an hour on maybe only ten minutes. When we were at our Aunt's house or with our grandparents, we had prayers every night before bed. My grandfather would read from the Bible, and then he would pray. Grandmother's head would tilt back, her mouth would open, and she would snore quietly as he prayed. We thought that was hilarious. Now I feel solidarity with her.

When I was fourteen I found a sweet letter I'd written to someone when I was younger. Struck by the contrast between my current inward edgy fourteen-year-old self and the sweetness of the kid I'd been, I started to cry. My dad noticed, and sat on the stairs with me, his arm around me, and prayed with me that the sweetness would come back. I tried, but I was fourteen, at a time when inner sweetness is intermittent at best.

Every morning Mama would wake up at five and start her prayers. I know she prayed for my sister and me, for my dad, for the kids in her second grade class. She found an enormous bottle of vodka deep in my fifteen year old sister's closet. She prayed about it, after pouring out the vodka. Years later she asked my sister about it. "Oh yeah, whatever happened to that bottle"? my sister asked. "I stuck it in my closet because I didn't know what to do with it. I won it at an employee raffle when I was a cashier at Geraldi's Market." She would pray for an hour and then practice her violin. That was my alarm clock. Every morning I woke up to scratchy Hanon exercises. She never got better, but she loved it, and she played in the neighborhood symphony in the back row and had a grand time. This brought home the lesson that a thing worth doing is worth doing badly, if it's fun.

My mother found a lump in her breast and began praying about it. For a year she told no one, and didn't go see a doctor. When the lump was starting to poke out so you could see it, she finally called a doctor. This makes me so angry. At whom?

Mama? The people who taught her how to be a Christian? How plain can it be that bad theology kills?

She went to a doctor who was understandably upset that she'd waited that long. This was the 70s, when treatments were available but harsh. She kept praying during the five years of her illness. Friends, churches, neighbors were asked to pray. I'm glad they prayed for her. Toward the end she asked the ministers from my dad's father's old church, Tenth Presbyterian. Our liberal ministers were abandoned in her trouble. The ones she gathered around her at the end were a Messianic Jewish Presbyterian minister and some others. I remember him particularly because he gave us a solemn talk before we started, saying that doubt could affect prayer's effectiveness, and that, if any among us had an iota of doubt that this prayer circle for her healing would work, we should leave the room immediately so our doubt would not infect the prayers. I was twenty-three, in seminary, as full of doubts and questions as any seminarian. I left the room. It still makes me feel like cussing. I got to be with her the night she died, though. I didn't pray that night, but I paid attention. It was the best I could do.

Do I pray now? Yes, I do. My prayers do not ask someone above me for something. It's not like God sits by, arms crossed, saying "I could help you, but I won't help you until you ask. Even then, you must ask correctly, with the right mixture of praise, supplication, gratitude and awe. Get it just right and I may help you." I only pray about little things, parking places, timing of things, knowledge of what to say in difficult situations, strength, and patience.

I prayed, in my way, for seven months as I sat in an orthopedic recliner. I would recover, start getting up on crutches or a walker, doing a little PT, and then go under the knife again and start all over. For seven months I dealt with the pain, with the opiates, getting on them, getting off, getting on, getting off. Healing and fighting despair took all my time and energy. I was lucky that I had a planned sabbatical coming up in a few months, so we just moved it up and I took all my sick days, burned the sabbatical, and then came back to work.

I guess feeling lucky depends on how you look at things. Luckiest would have been not to have gotten an infection. Luckiest would have been that they didn't damage my femoral nerve during the third surgery, so now I live with a clumsy numb foot and an unstable knee. Is it temporary? I hope so. We'll see. From my recliner I could make out a face in one of the swirly shades on the lights of the ceiling fan. It looked like a face in a Chinese ink painting, long mustache, eyes closed, a look of anguish, as if he were also in pain. I called him my pain angel, and I would talk to him. I didn't ask for anything, I just talked, crying sometimes. When I was alone in the house I would wail to him. Is that what prayer is, just talking to hear what's happening inside, acknowledging that you aren't able to get through this thing just staying inside your own head? I don't know. That doesn't sound right to me.

The religious people I hang around with say prayer is just a way of reminding yourself that you aren't alone. Are you not? Why not just talk to the people you love who are there ready to help you? They say prayer helps you get your thoughts in order. Ok. So does writing or, see above, talking to the people you love. They say prayer is more for you than for God. Yeah. If God is the kind of God I was raised to believe in he doesn't need anything from anyone. He is the one who gives, not the one who is given to, but the God I believe in needs to be loved and talked to. Because s/he is love, and s/he is a loving listener. I'm not sure which pronouns the Divine Mystery prefers.

Here is how I think about what I call God. As I began telling you before, I think that love lasts, the energy of love lasts in the universe, in a way that the energy of other things do not. Every loving interaction since the beginning of beings, a mama whale for her calf, a papa gorilla for his partner, every loving human interaction throughout time adds to the stream of the energy of love that flows in and around the universe like an immense river. So this love, that I would call god, can be added to by my actions. If I throw love at someone, if I comfort or listen or reach out to another being. the energy of that love augments god. Prayer, in this case, is participation. I participate with god and god flows through me with love and accompanies me with love in all I do, in all that happens to me.

Kiya

ॐ

During those months, my wondrous wife was right there, taking care of everything. My gratitude for her perseverance, her grace, sturdy love, her honor and her fierce determination all combine to dazzle me daily.

We met at a Unitarian Universalist summer family camp and became friends. They housed all of the musicians on one hall in one dorm, I suppose so we wouldn't drive everyone else crazy. One summer we dreamed up a temporary band called the Divas of Mercy. She was Diva Spike. I was Diva Stevie, twirling and saying benedictory things. We bonded, smoking air cigarettes. What's that? I sometimes pretend I'm smoking, in rock n roll situations. Leaning against a wall next to each other, she saw what I was doing and, snapping her fingers, holding her thumb up to my imaginary cigarette, she offered me an imaginary light. I had never found someone who would play air cigarettes with me until that moment. Traveling home from that camp, I realized something big had happened. I didn't want to tell her, though. I thought I would go home and talk myself out of it. Falling in love would have been very inconvenient for all concerned. It turns out she felt something big had happened too, but was trying to get over it as well. Love blossomed and grew, and we finally talked to each other about it. After a while, she moved in with me and my younger son in South Carolina. When we'd been together six years or so, we decided to get married. I was afraid to do it, worried that I'd been unable to keep my first marriage commitment. . She wrote me a song called "Icarus," about putting on our wings and having courage. "Yeah, everyone knows he fell. That's the part they tell. But something else is true. Before he fell, he flew." What melted, with that song, was my resistance to making promises again, my certainty that I was not good marriage material.

In late December we were riding the train all along the Texas border, on our way to California for a Christmas visit. It was Christmas Eve in the dining car, somewhere near El Paso. I made a ring out of the foil from a baked potato and asked her to marry me. We eloped, which was much less terrifying to me than planning a big wedding. Along with that, we didn't want anyone there who would have complicated feelings about us marrying. My family is a lovely bunch, but I didn't know that they would have been all for us. Her family is all gone; she is the last one left.

We found a silversmith in the back of a Latin grocery who sold us two rings. Our younger son, the one we were visiting, sang "I will always love you," by the Cure. He was joined by Kiya's oldest friend, a tall lion of a woman who was in Kiya's first band, back when they were fifteen. Our older son and his wife attended via Skype, and they had a reading. We were out by the ocean, with night falling. Dockweiler Beach State Park was dotted with lit fire circles, all the way down the beach. The waves rolled in, sounding the way they had sounded forever. It was New Year's Eve, so fireworks celebrated our vows. Drifting over our heads was music from a nearby bar, where a Doors cover band sang "Don't you love her madly"? It was a perfect wedding for us. We spent the night at the Cadillac Hotel off the Venice Beach Boardwalk.

When we got home, we had a big party, It was Scottish themed, since we were going to honeymoon in Edinburgh the next summer, and all the church folks came to dance with us.

Kiya has been a professional road musician, a singer-songwriter, since she was in her early twenties. Her band, Stealin' Horses, hit it big in the 80s, with her hit "Turnaround." You can still find their MTV video on YouTube. She's kept her music going ever since then.

She had to stop touring during the time I was injured, and that was a big change for her. She'd come off the road once before, to take care of and support her grandparents as they died of cancer. She decided, as I got better, that she would go to seminary to become a UU minister. She found a non-residential program at Starr King School for the Ministry in Berkeley, California. She would have to be there for some time every January and every August. We both loved the people who run the place, and it turned out to be just what she needed. It was quite different from music graduate school. Mysteries and arcane knowledge were being taught in both places, but in seminary it felt more like they wanted to welcome you into the guild, rather than making you run the gauntlet to gain admission. Now she combines the music and ministry paths as the director of The People's Orchestra of Austin, where you can come play whatever you want to play, at whatever level of skill you have, and she will arrange a part for you in a Mozart piece, a Bruno Mars or Blues or Led Zeppelin piece, and it will sound good. I love watching the people blossom as they find their music and become a member of the band.

Jesus in the Doorway

ॐ

I used to go with her to California for school. We'd get an Air BnB. She'd go to class and I'd go to a coffee shop to write. I liked a place on San Pablo Avenue called Highwire, because the atmosphere was simple, the people seemed friendly, and there were lots of electrical outlets, which signals to writers that we are welcome. As I'm writing this, during the pandemic, I'm listening to an eight-hour recording of some coffee shop. I hear the hiss of the espresso machine, I hear "Josh? Josh? Your latte is here at the counter."

I hear a nice-sounding man tell the barista that someone left something behind at their table. Coffee beans are ground, cabinet doors slam.

As I fed the parking meter in the rain one January day on San Pablo Avenue in Berkeley, a man lying in a nearby doorway was talking to me. He was the picture of misery. What drew my eye were his crutches. I've used crutches in my life, off and on, and they are a pain. I'm grateful for them, and they feel like a kindness, but I prefer being able to do without them. One thing about being on crutches is that it's hard to get up from the floor by yourself if your legs don't work. The man talking to me was covered with a heavy moving-company blanket, and it was soaked. He had a pizza box in front of him with two crusts in it. I'd already decided to give him five dollars. That's unusual for me. Usually I don't give to beggars. I call them that because that's what one of the men without homes who come to my church said I should call them. "They're different from us with no homes," Mike said, "there's homeless, and there's beggars."

I tried to give the man the five, but what he was saying finally sank in. "I can't get up," he said. "I've been here all night. I'm wet. Just waiting for the sun."

"We're going to have to wait two more days for sun, the weather says," I told him.

"I can't get up, and my bag here spilled and got pee all over me and my pizza." I focused, and his urostomy bag was lying there on the sidewalk. "Can you just get me some coffee? I can't get up, you see."

"Black, or cream and sugar"? I asked.

"Plenty of cream and sugar," he said.

I went into the coffee shop and got him a large coffee, choosing randomly between the two fancy roasts they were offering. "This one is a bit more earthy," the barista said. I got him a chocolate muffin too. Pouring a good amount of raw sugar in with as much half and half as would fit, I took the food and drink to him. I tried to give him the five again, but he waved me off.

"I've got an extra dollar if you need it," he said. That's the part that made me want to cry. "I love you!" He called all the way down the sidewalk as I walked away. "Two more days 'til sun!" he called out, as I waved and laughed. I should have said "I love you too," but I didn't. The stories from my childhood religion say that was Jesus, or an angel. Could be. Jesus certainly showed himself willing to endure depths of pain and discomfort on this planet to show solidarity with the beings here.

My current religion makes me want to despise myself for this whole story. White lady gives beggar some food, and it moves her. Should I instead have told him that I was engaged in resisting capitalism and the structures of injustice that propelled him into that doorway? Tell him that and give him five dollars? The writer of the Book of James says "If you say 'Go in peace, be warm and well fed,' but you don't do anything about their physical needs, what good is it"? So I'm glad I could give him what he asked for without a diatribe against capitalism. It's not either or, I know. I can work for justice and reach out as an individual to do a kindness.

How do I not despise myself for saying that the man gave me a gift in this interaction? He gave me conversation, told me he loved me, and offered me a dollar. When I am even a little miserable I get cranky. If I were on the ground unable to get up, hungry, thirsty, using crutches, soaking wet with rain and pee, I can't even tell you how far I would be from offering anyone a dollar, much less telling them that I loved them.

I wish I'd been up to offering to get him up off the wet sidewalk. If I had, we'd both be soaked with rain and pee and we'd both need crutches.

I know that feeling that I should despise myself for this white lady moment is wrong. I don't think I do the planet any good when I'm covered in shame. When this tangle tightens, I remember hearing about the Sisters who work with street children in one of the barrios in Managua. My Aunt Dorothy, who worked with the barrio kids as well, asked them "How do you go on, knowing there are more children than you can help, knowing this pain will go on and on"?

The Sisters replied, "We go on and on as well."

What I Learned from My Therapy Clients

ॐ

Therapy was a wonderful life work for a while. I adored almost all my clients. I honor them so much for their insights, their struggles, their courage and their persistence. They taught me, and I got to savor the pearls of wisdom they shared, their quirky ways of describing things and the ways they dealt with the bad things and share what worked with the next ones to come along.

South Carolina is in the middle of the "incest belt." Fundamentalist religion, they say, contributes to the father's sense of ownership of the family, a king-like power combined with the crazy-making knowledge that he doesn't really know how to make all the decisions. Combine that with attendance at a church where the preacher tells parents they are responsible for their children's souls, and that beating them is a good way to make sure they don't go bad. Undergird it all with the worship of a father-God who, according to the way that preacher tells the story, killed his own child to fulfill a rule he himself set up. It gives people a twisted view of what a father is.

Abused and broken folks, poisoned by toxic versions of religion, washed up one by one on the shores of my therapy office. I tried to keep my inner shields up, but years of stories of tyranny and horror inside childhood homes traumatized me vicariously.

That's one side-effect of working as a listener that we didn't hear about during my training. I understand they talk about it more now. I would drive home at night looking at the lit-up homes along the road, picturing terrors and despair behind every door.

The kind of therapy I'd been taught was a combination of deep listening, silence, asking good questions and teaching communication techniques for couples. People would have insights about why they did certain things, why they set up certain situations in their lives over and over again, but those insights, mysteriously, didn't seem to have much effect. Much later we began understanding that trauma, is held in the body, how trauma reactions are so deep and quick that they bypass the rational thinking process altogether. So rational therapy, while it can have good effects, can't completely help the body heal from those experiences. By the time therapists began to understand those things I was burned out, internally injured, unable to do couples counseling because I'd lost my belief in marriage.

I pulled an Animal Medicine card one day, and the reading said I'd been working with Snake medicine. Snake medicine is when a healer gets bitten, poisoned, and then internally transmutes the poison into something that is good medicine for others. That sure did describe how I had been feeling. Bitten, poisoned by the stories of trauma I heard day in and day out, taking the stories in and working with them to transmute the poison into something beneficial for my clients. I was weary.

These days I don't sit as quietly. Preaching, counseling as a minister, writing songs, columns, and books, are the ways I share what I've learned so far. And I give talks at conferences of nurses, librarians, and other educators. I mainly gave a talk called "Your Surly Inner Waitress' Guide to Life." This is how it goes:

Your Surly Inner Waitress' Guide to Life

The first thing I want to say is that, while I know of all of these things to do to handle life, I don't always do them. I'm still learning. If you meet someone who says they have it all together, run as fast as you can the other way. People can have it all together for a short time, then something falls apart, and they don't have it together any more. There seem to be people who think that there is some state of grace, some state of wondrous mental health, where you can float through anything that goes wrong with no pain at all, with your yard mowed, your windows washed, your sidewalks shoveled, and your tank full of gas. That's crazy. Life is painful, difficult, confusing, joyful, ecstatic, and boring. Mentally healthy people feel distressed when bad things happen. We have all met people who are presenting themselves as so spiritual and at peace that they are a total pain to be around. That CAN'T be right. They talk in soft tones, wide-eyed, and they don't blink much. It feels more like they are performing peace of mind than actually living it. All that said, let's get to your surly inner waitress, who practices some techniques you might find useful!

The limits of what life will pile on you, in large part, are yours to determine. I remember waiting tables as a young woman, struggling to give good service to my tables of customers. If I had too many tables, no one got the best service. Everyone ends up frustrated. Some waitresses get surly when folks don't understand this. I tried my best to be sweet to everyone. That didn't guarantee they'd be sweet back to me, though. One of the veteran waitresses we all admired for her skill would keep her feet moving, balancing plates on both arms, and, if someone across the room waved an empty coffee mug in her direction, she'd say in a scratchy voice, "Sorry Hon, not my table."

In my life, I figure I have a certain number of tables for which I'm responsible: my family, my work, myself, and a couple of volunteer things. When someone asks me to do something else, and it feels like an empty coffee mug at a table for which I'm not responsible, I just keep my feet moving, my plates balanced, and say "Sorry Hon, not my table."

You can stop trying to make everybody happy.

It would be such a lovely world if everyone were to admire you, be happy with all your decisions, applaud the direction in which you take your life, not fuss, not worry, and feel inspired by your example. I'm tempted to giggle, just writing this. Your actual job, rather than making people happy, is to create a situation in which they could be happy if they chose to be. This is especially good to remember when you are on a long car trip with children or living with teenagers.

You know from experience, though, that certain people are more comfortable being unhappy. They may feel that too much happiness is dangerous, that they are tempting fate if they get too comfortable, that intelligent people must be too aware of the world's sorrows to feel happiness, or that being happy makes a person silly or vulnerable to disappointment. It could be that they are among the natural systems analysts in the world, hard-wired to look at a scene or a process and pick out what is wrong. At a gorgeous meal they will comment only on the soup that is over salted. On a home tour they will focus their attention on the one place the painter smudged on a window sill. We need these people, and we might imagine that they feel and express happiness in other ways than we do.

Walk toward criticism

There's a saying in the South: "If one person calls you an ass, shake it off. When two or three people tell you you're an ass, start shopping for a saddle."

We can grow through "notes" on our performance or our person. There is such a thing as constructive criticism, given from love. Painful as that is, it can be a good idea to listen to it. If you get the same notes from a variety of people, you will want to take that seriously to see if there is something you'd like to do differently. There is no pleasant criticism, and a lot of it tells you more about the critic than about what is being criticized. Some people criticize because they love you and they want the best for you. Some are simply in the habit of criticizing, and they do it to everyone and everything, which is why they are doing it to you. Other people do it to make themselves feel stronger by making you feel smaller.

Walking toward the criticism will help you discern which is which. When someone says something to you, ask them to tell you more. If they have been thinking about you, about something you need to know, they will be able to say more in order to help you. If you pursue someone who is just trying to break you down, they probably won't be able to say more. Their plan was to hit and run, to deliver the poison and watch you fall over. If you ask them to say more about it, they will probably start to stammer and hedge, obfuscate with vagueness and get away from you as fast as they can. I call this their "squid ink" defense. When a squid is threatened it squirts out an inky cloud behind which it can escape. By the time the water clears again, they're nowhere to be found. When people feel like they are losing an argument or being found out as having nothing of substance to say, they just start spewing out words about anything that comes to mind. They just want to make a thick enough cloud between the two of you so they can slink away to a safer distance.

Take control of what you can

You already know this. Some things can be controlled and some can't. I believe with my whole heart in controlling what I can. That is a comfortable place for me. Some people have called me a control freak (I prefer "control aficionado"), and I think it's an honorable role. But people can't be controlled. You can't make people do right. You can try, but it takes an incredible investment of time and money or violence to control people. You have tried, but you may never be able to get your brother to achieve his potential. Your parents may always bail out your baby sister when she gets into financial trouble, even though they agree with you that it's not the best thing for her. That guy who sits in the next cubicle is totally making everyone else in the office carry him, and you may not be able to bring it to anyone's attention without looking like a crank.

You can try to influence people with your words or your actions. They may be inspired by your example; they may take your hints, but they may never notice at all. I remember the *I Ching* talking about how sometimes the "window of influence" is open, and it is at that time that what you say or do can make a difference. Then the window slams shut, and you're wasting your time if you try to have any influence at that point.

It is important to say your piece once or, at most, twice, and then subside. After that, the other person knows what you're going to say. If the other person is your child, rest assured that they carry your voice inside them at all times, whether you are there or not. They know what you think about things. They know your words. They know, more importantly, how you act.

Your children will turn out pretty much like you, if you are the one who reared them, so if you want them to be great people, the thing to do is become a great person yourself, which will improve their odds. Of course, as Plato supposedly said, sometimes golden parents have silver children, and sometimes silver parents have golden children. As I write that, I realize how impossible it is to tell one from the other sometimes.

If you don't simply speak your mind once or maybe twice, if you keep hammering at someone, a relationship forms between the mule that lives inside everyone and your words, so that when you say it again and again, their inner mule wakes up and digs in. Picture the mule with its stubborn hoofs stuck in its stubborn ears, singing "Blalalalala" as you talk. Nearly everyone, along with having an inner mule, has an inner voice of wisdom. Sometimes it's very faint, but if you keep talking, they won't be able to hear their own inner wisdom for all the yak yak yak and bla la la.

Words aren't the only way of influencing a situation. I heard about a woman who got tired of nagging her husband to pick his clothes up off of the floor, so she picked them all up every day and stuffed them into his pillow case. That's non-verbal communication right there. When my kids wouldn't help me with chores, and later they would ask for a ride to the mall, I would shrug and tell them I understood from how they'd acted that we weren't helping each other that day. If you have a friend or a spouse who won't/can't change even after you've asked from your heart, you have a decision to make. Stay or go. Leaving can be a powerful communication tool.

Or change yourself. Any of those three are valid choices.

What you think of me is none of my business

Another matter you have little control over is what other people think of you. You try to live your life the best way you can, but sometimes you will be misunderstood, misrepresented, or misperceived. "What you think of me is none of my business." That's another thing I stole straight from the twelve-steppers. When my boys were teens, they were excruciatingly easy to embarrass. If I would sing while driving, one would hiss "MOM! Stop singing. Those other people think you're weird."

"Those people coming by us in the other lane, each of us going over forty-five miles an hour? That's a total of ninety miles an hour we're traveling past each other. They're looking over here, identifying me, identifying you, perceiving that I'm singing, and thinking I'm weird"?

"Just stop singing, please, Mom."

"What they think of me is none of my business." This came in handy when I came out as gay in the 90s in our small southern town. I knew people would be thinking all kinds of things about me. I was a minister. I had been a minister's wife. I was the mother of two children. My job had been as one of the main couple's counselors in that town. I had quit that part of my practice when I ended my marriage, because it didn't feel very therapeutic to be doing that work while feeling the way I was feeling about marriage. As I've told you, some people actually turned their backs on my when we met at the grocery store. Other people were fine. Mostly people watch for you to give them clues about how to treat you. Another element that's very difficult to control is yourself. Some people say they know how to do that, but I'm dubious. We can try to influence others, say what we have to say and then stop, and we can try to control ourselves, but that is about the limit of it.

How to help others

First of all, wait until they ask you for help. Many of us are wired to pick up other people's problems as soon as they tell us about them, which is disrespectful to them. It's as if we feel that they've come and dumped a problem in our lap, so we're obliged to take it and try to solve it. Do not do this right away, even if you can. Take time to say something like "That sure is a problem, what are you going to do"? Another good question is "What have you already tried"?

Also, don't help when helping isn't going to help. You can pour effort, love and time into some people and it all just runs out the hole in their spirits as fast as you pour it in. They're not helped, and you become a dried-out dishrag. Be very careful about giving advice. No one really wants it. Even when they pay you an enormous amount of money for an hour of your time, and they ask what they should do, they don't really want to hear it.

Focus on the people who can benefit most from your help

In my training as a family therapist, we were taught that you can influence a family most profoundly by working most intensely with the people in the family who are the healthiest. Most families have a person who seems to have the most problems. This person is called the "identified patient." They are doing a good job, because they have brought the family in for some help. You help the family a lot by working with its healthiest people on their transformation. The health then ripples out from those people into the family system and the whole family gets better. In your life, you are surrounded by people who seem to be in various degrees of trouble. Some people are in so much trouble that they could take everything you've got and it would barely make a dent in their troubles. They would be a tiny smidge better for five minutes, and you would be decimated. That is not a good use of resources. Other people need what you've got, what you can give easily. You won't be too depleted and they will benefit from what you've done. This is what you want to try for.

Learn to accept help

Don't be hard to help. Some people get so crabby when they have to be helped. They are used to being the helpers, and it feels weak or embarrassing to need help from someone else. This is most likely to happen when a powerful helping person becomes sick or elderly. They need help but they've had absolutely no practice in the receiving of it. They get grumpy or ashamed, peevish or embarrassed, so giving them any help is doubly difficult. You not only have to help them, you have to reassure them at the same time that it's fine, that you don't mind helping. You not only have to give the help but you have to endure their crabby embarrassment at the same time. Practice receiving help gracefully when you are younger and healthier. Then, if you get sick or elderly, you will be a pleasure to help rather than a pain.

Do what you want to do. Don't do what you don't want to do.

This is simple to say, but complicated to do. It sounds hedonistic, but not if you take the long view. You have goals, and in order to attain those goals, certain things should be done. You don't want to do your homework, but you do it because you want to graduate. You want to graduate because you would like to increase your odds of being strong in the world as your life progresses. You don't want to go to the doctor, but you go, because you want your body to be healthy so you can do the things you'd like to do to have joy in your life. Sometimes you do things you don't want to do in order to get to something you do want. Other times you are asked to do what you don't want to do, and there's no reason to do it. Or the reason you would do it is to keep someone else happy. Then you ask yourself whether your unhappiness is worth their happiness. Will it make you unhappy at an eight on a scale of one-to-ten, and will it only make them happy a two out of ten? Not worth it, then. Will it only make you unhappy a three out of ten and it will make them happy a nine? Worth it. Unless it's every hour of every day. Then the day-by-day willingness of the other person for you to be unhappy becomes an issue to be examined.

If you do things that make you unhappy, uneasy, miserable or conflicted as part of your job, it's time to wonder whether this is the job for you. If the reason you're doing something is for the money, ask yourself what you want the money for. Money is nothing by itself: you can't eat it, it can't keep you safe. You buy things with it. Security, in a limited way, health, mobility, status, the ability to help people, adventure, whatever it is on your list. So figure out what it is that you are after at the end of the process. If it's adventure, you may not need as much money as you think you do. If it's security, you may find other ways to feel safe. Does that make sense? I'm all for making money, but it's good to know why you want it.

Honor your anger

Anger is a good signal that your boundaries have been violated. It's time to move yourself in some direction, or to push back against the violation, if you are able. Good anger, fruitful anger, helps you change the situation. You don't want to wallow in it, no matter how great it feels to be in the role of righteous and innocent victim. Your anger is telling you to make a change. It's like the heat on a stove burner. It can cook things for you, transforming situations like heat transforms ingredients in a stew, or it can burn your house down if it gets mishandled. Anger can be great transformative energy, and you should let yourself get good at it.

Here is something else to think about. Sometimes a good portion of my anger is anger at myself. I should have known something, or I did know and put myself into a bad position anyway. Maybe I made a bad decision, or I did something I knew was wrong. So I'm angry at myself. Anyway, getting that question asked and answered gets you some distance toward resolving the situation.

A related, terrifying, tricky question

I would never ask anyone this question directly, but it's a question I hold in mind while listening to someone, and it's a question I ask myself when I have the courage. That question is "is there anything this problem is doing for me"? Maybe if I didn't have this problem I would have to change my picture of myself and my life. That's a lot of trouble. Maybe if I didn't have this problem people would expect more of me, or I would expect more of myself. I do not believe that we create our own reality, or that you should blame people for the problems they're having — those are fruitless and cruel avenues to pursue. I've just noticed in my life that sometimes I'll be dealing with a problem, a resentment, a habit, a dilemma, that is actually doing something for me. As soon as I have that realization, I have to decide what to do about it. Mostly I just try to put it out of my mind, because change is hard!

Watching skull cinema

I had a client who used to say "I was up all night watching skull cinema." She was having conversations in her head rather than having them with the actual people.

Skull cinema is exhausting and, unless you are rehearsing for a real conversation, it's pretty fruitless.

Take your sails out of their wind

Some people live in your head, and some of them live in your life too. You feel their disapproval, or you want their attention and affirmation. It drives you crazy, seeing their blank or unhappy face when you do something you thought was really good. You can feel their opinions about your clothes or your hair or your job or your parenting style or the music you listen to or the art you make. The vibe from them is a constant wind, blowing your little sail boat around on the lake in patterns that don't feel good. Here is the solution. Picture yourself furling your sails when that wind starts blowing you all over the place. If you take your sails out of their wind, they can huff and puff and try to blow you all over the place, but it won't have much effect on you.

If someone, say, an ex, keeps harassing you, criticizing you, sending you awful emails, wanting long grueling phone conversations where they tell you what a terrible person you are, understand that you don't have to be part of that. You can hang up the phone or forward the emails to a friend so they can tell you if there is anything there you might actually need to know.

Self-care beyond the bubble bath

In the magazines people write that you should take care of yourself by taking baths, lighting candles, and other gentle things. Those ideas are grand, but taking care of yourself also means making sure you are being paid enough for the work you do so that you can be strong in the world. Taking care of yourself means having good boundaries so you can say "I can't listen to you if you speak to me that way," or "Take your hand off of my shoulder," or "No, I'm not going to read the pornography you wrote and tell you what I think about it, and no, I don't want to see a picture of your penis."

Accept who you are

Some of us were brought up with a religion that described us as miserable sinners, unable to choose anything right. Some grew up with parents who thought if they said anything good about you, you'd turn out badly. Some had people around who thought everything you did was great, so you never really know if what you do is ok or not. Self-acceptance, to some people, feels dangerous. Who knows what you might turn into if you accepted yourself for who you are? Self-acceptance doesn't necessarily mean loving each and every quality that is inside you. Some of our qualities are healthy and fun — others are destructive. Knowing and accepting the unhealthy mean or hateful parts of yourself is important too. Carl Jung called those qualities your "shadow." If you try to pretend they aren't there, you will be using a lot of energy and feeling a lot of stress trying to keep them denied and hidden. It's like being in the room with a wasp. You want to know where it is, otherwise you might sit on it by accident and get stung.

Choose to enjoy your life

In many situations you have a choice in whether or not to enjoy what's happening. You can zone out during the drive to work or you can sing to the radio or have a running contest for the most interesting looking person you pass on the road. You can fume through the meeting or you can think about how you would explain the interactions you're seeing to a visitor from Venus. Have fun when you can. I sometimes go too far with that one. I had just decided to try to have fun in any situation where that is possible, and I was being the guest preacher at a tiny Presbyterian church in a country town. The choir sang, and a soloist sang a beautiful thing in Spanish. When they finished and sat down, I stood up, and said. "It's always lovely to hear such beautiful music, and so enjoyable to find out they speak in tongues in Presbyterian churches!" The choir gasped and the soloist whisper-hissed at me, "It was *Spanish.*"

Part of enjoying your life is enjoying your body. Wear things that are comfortable. Have great sex if you can. Learn about your body, talk about it, and quit hating it and starving it and being ashamed of it.

Watch your language

One thing I know is that you should speak to yourself kindly. Name-calling and imprecations of worthlessness are unhelpful at best, and harmful at worst. I've been shocked at the nastiness of the way some people speak to themselves. They scoff at the thought that they should speak to themselves sweetly. "Maybe call yourself sweetie-pie, or honeybunch," I suggest, and they laugh, disbelieving. When I learned that I should speak to myself kindly, it was fairly easy for me to begin. As a child I had the extreme good fortune to be raised by people who spoke to me gently. No names were called, no predictions of worthlessness or failure. They believed in me so I believed in myself. Other people were raised much less gently. Some were spoken to harshly, others were barely spoken to at all.

I was spoken to gently, but there is a hell-on-wheels critical inner voice ragging on everything I think and do. I've spent lots of time teaching people to recognize and name the Inner Critic. In one workshop I led, a man told me with tears in his eyes that he had been thinking the voice of the Critic in his head was God. Knowing that it wasn't God who was poking him about every real and imagined flaw was an enormous relief. My Critic is energetic, tireless. "You don't know what you're talking about. You look silly when you wear that. You are too angry. You aren't angry enough." I wish I remembered who suggested that I create for my Critic an imagined classroom full of intelligent students who would listen to whatever he said, taking notes and nodding. I now put him in the classroom next to where I am and let him tell the students how awful I am while I get on with what I'm doing. They listen with rapt attention and take notes. He is happy.

I've worked with hundreds of people in my life, as a minister, a therapist, a speaker and a workshop leader. Almost all of us have the Critic inside, and almost all of us have a certain amount of anxiety about the tasks and interactions we will be faced with, day-to-day. One person, at the start of a joint project, said "This is going to be easy, safe, and fun!" I was agog. My approach had usually been more along the lines of "Ok, this is going to be hard, but we can do it. We can pay attention and be careful and do everything right and it will work out." Easy, safe, and fun? Was that sacrilegious? I mean, in some secular way? I confess I've tried it on occasion since then. My inner woman doesn't believe it, but the sheer audacity of reminding myself that I could think of a project or a task that way makes me laugh and reminds me that when I have an anxious and dour view, it's my choice.

The Critic accuses, melodramatically, "You've done nothing your whole life but teach things that are easy for you." I have to have court inside my mind, bringing to the bench examples of things I teach that I am still wrestling with, things I may never completely understand. The Inner Defense Attorney says that most teachers teach things they know, and when they've put in their ten thousand hours on something, of course it's easier for them than it is for the people they're teaching. Piano teachers don't teach Greek, and Greek professors don't teach surfing, as a general rule. The Critic is shown by the bailiffs to his classroom, where his students open their laptops, ready to attend to his bloviations.

Preachers preach about the things they themselves need to hear. Look out if your preacher jumps up and down on sexual behavior every Sunday, because you know that is what's on their mind. Teachers teach things that interest them, or things they've spent thousands of hours studying, living, developing, and exploring. My Critic pops his head out of the door of the classroom to bellow at me "Dilettante!" He thinks I know a bit about too many things. That's the job though. One Sunday you're preaching history, the next, about managing anger, something you learned from Buddhism after that, and then a Bible story. I have had the experience, after a service, of being corrected by mathematicians, by physicists, astronomers, historians, and neurobiologists. You talk to people about all of the things a life can hold, and the variety is immense. I hear stories. I tell stories, I write stories. Those are the building blocks of my world. I say to myself, "Just teach and write about what you know, sweetie-pie." To my red-faced, bug-eyed Critic, trying to stare me down from the doorway of his classroom, I say "Thanks, Honeybunch!"

Take power in your life.

No one who has power will give you any. You are going to have to take it. People will find all kinds or reasons for you not to change the way things are. They will throw the word "selfish " at you, they will say you are mean, they will tell you no one will like you any more if you start making decisions for your life. Even the word "power" is scary to us. The main powerful women we see on TV are the skinny ones with long fingernails who make other people's lives miserable. Let's see, what powerful women did I see as a child? There was Maleficent, the wicked fairy in Sleeping Beauty. You wouldn't want to be like her. The good fairies had power but they used it to clean up the house and make Beauty a dress and a birthday cake. I didn't really want to be like them. I liked Wonder Woman, and Emma Peele of the Avengers. I long to own and use a lasso of truth nearly every day. Find some powerful women you like and ask yourself what it is about them that you want to incorporate into your way of doing things.

Be a quitter

If you are in a bad situation, try to get out of it. Many of us were raised not to be quitters, and it is important to give things a chance. However, some of us hang on to bad situations way too long because we don't want to be seen as quitters. No one stands outside a burning building and yells at the people running out, screaming "Quitters! Quitters!"

You don't have to be right all the time

If you have the ability to say, "I could be wrong," or "You could be right," you will get rid of some unnecessary stress. No one is right all the time. Not even your dad. Make room in your day for mistakes. You are going to make them. Why not make room for them in your plan? Life gets easier if you can say. "I'm sorry, that was my mistake. And it won't be the last one." Of course I understand that, for those of you in the medical professions, you can't make mistakes at work. Just try to learn to change gears when you go into the rest of your day, so you don't feel that you have to be right everywhere and all the time.

Make a practice of gratitude

So many of us are so stressed about what we don't have that we miss what we do have. We are uncomfortable with our bodies so we don't use them or have good sex or enjoy food or participate in activities that are fun. Be grateful for your body and what it can do. Some of us are so stressed about not having enough money that we are trying all kinds of things to get more. That's fine, but notice how rich you are. You have hot water that comes out of a tap right in your kitchen. You have a machine to wash clothes for you. You have a mind, a heart, and imagination. That is a lot.

Know what your responsibilities are and what they aren't.

This whole speech began with the Surly Inner Waitress. She knows she is responsible for this many tables. She can keep this many tables served, but if she starts trying to take care of table that are not hers she gets frazzled and can't do a good job of the responsibilities that are hers. So when someone waves her down for coffee, she says, "Sorry Hon, not my table," and keeps walking. We need to be clear about what is our responsibility, what is our business, and what is not. If someone waves us down with a problem that is not ours to take on, an appropriate response is: remember? "Wow. That sure is a problem. What are you going to do about it"? This honors both the person with the problem and it honors your own time and good will. If you can help, and if your help will actually help, then go for it. We all need to be helpers for one another, but we don't want to be compulsive helpers. There is wisdom and skill in knowing the difference.

Also, please remember that you are not the only helper in the world, or even the only one in the room where you sit. The Creative is always at work and at play in the world, and the Creative has many ways to help in any situation. If you have ever sung in a choir, you know that, when the music calls for a long sustained note, the singers breathe at different times so that the note continues. If you need to take time to breathe, someone else will keep the note going. We're in this together.

Thank you for inviting me, and letting me tell you all of these things you already knew!

If I Were To Make Up My Own Religion

ॐ

Once, long ago, in a confrontation about how people in my Unitarian Universalist congregation celebrate Easter, someone sneered, "So, if you all don't believe in the bodily resurrection of Jesus, what do you have, just pretty yellow flower day"? That has stuck with me. My first response, in my head, was "your mama's a pretty yellow flower." I felt shamed by what they'd said at first, as if being inspired by flower, a symbol of resurrection and new life, was weaker and less grounded than believing in the literal historical resurrection of a person's body. There are lots of stories around the world and throughout history of dying and rising gods. Those stories are a way of talking about the absolute miracle of the dying and rising of the wheat, the corn, the pretty yellow flowers. They speak of how the food we count on falls into the ground and seems to die, then grows again and produces what keeps the planet alive. Dying and rising is one of the most basic motions of life on our planet.

Living things are full of the life force, which urges: "Make more life! Spread your seed! Survive!" Flowers do that by attracting animals and humans through their beauty, their usefulness, their ability to help with pain, changing consciousness, or forgetting. In early hunting and gathering days, flowers appearing in a place would signal to the gatherers that soon there would appear in that place tubers or fruits, something to eat, and that they should return to that place soon.

Other plants attract attention by being good medicine. They produce chemicals that help us, so they get eaten when an animal or a human has a stomach ache, or they are taken to someone to soothe a rash, and they are cared for and valued for their medicinal properties. The cannabis plant is being tended by the best gardeners of our time, who spend energy and money giving the plants everything they need, transporting them, cultivating them, making them stronger, moving them inside when the outside is inhospitable. What more could a plant want, if its drive is to propagate itself and increase its security?

I could do worse in my life than to emulate the pretty yellow flower. I would like to have a beauty in my spirit that attracts others with the promise of nourishment. I would like to be good medicine and good fun.

A medieval Christian mystic named Hildegarde of Bingen wrote: "the breath of the air makes the earth fruitful. Thus the air is the soul of the earth, moistening it, greening it." I see it as a green fire burning through all of the connected earth, through the grass, the trees, through us. Watching any spring unfurl I see that greening breath moving up slowly through the stems, sending energy through the tips of the leaves as they lift, gathering in what they need from the sun and sky.

I grow in cycles like the plants do. Sometimes I'm a winter spirit, where my branches look bare and all life has gone underground. I'm grieving or resting, ill, confused, or injured. I look out from my dark rest-place at people who are in a more summer spirit, lively and open, flourishing and at a peak of productivity, and, depending on how hungry, angry, lonely or tired I am, I might compare myself to them and find myself wanting.

A spring spirit, I think, has to do with blossoming. Blossoming is a time of big change. I used to have roses by my house in South Carolina that would bloom in the spring and keep blooming through November. I found myself wondering if it hurts to bloom. I know scientifically, that doesn't make sense, but suspend disbelief for a moment and picture this: if you were a rose, and this were your first time out, would you be having fun being a bud, all curled around yourself, feeling hugged and tight, knowing what's what? You are soaking up the sun, being gently tossed in warm wind, and suddenly everything starts to loosen up. Your petals are letting go! They are moving apart from one another! Do you try to hold on, try to grab for the edges and keep the changes from happening? Maybe you think to yourself, "I don't understand this, but maybe it's what's supposed to happen." You allow the once tight petals to move apart. Does it hurt? Does it cause anxiety? The roses seem to accept each stage with grace, but how do we really know that? Maybe we just can't hear them screaming.

The same green fire that shoots up the stem of a rose and causes it to bloom also drives the petals to open so far that they fall to the ground. The rose hip swells and turns red and bursts open, releasing the seeds of future roses. Is it any wonder that we tell stories of human blossoming, then growing wise, spreading our seeds, our deeds, our words, our offspring, then falling to the ground to lie still for a time before rising again? At this point in my life, my rosy bloom is finished, and I feel myself to be a rose hip, filled with seeds to share, glowing in the afternoon sun. We see the mystery all around us. Spirits winter over, and then spirits bloom. The same green fire drives it all, the Spirit of Life to which we in my faith community sing praises. What is more worthy of worship than this?

My made-up religion even has a theology of the afterlife.

I was thinking about death and greening one weekend camping with my friends. We were nestled in a clearing on a Carolina mountain side. Most of the folks were around the campfire, talking or dozing. Our chef was in the cooking tent grilling and gossiping with his girlfriend and a couple of others. He wasn't wearing his high heels that day. He does sometimes, but only on camping weekends. I love those people, and they love me. Being surrounded by love is a fine way to spend your time. I wandered off to the hammock, and lay there looking up at the sky through early April leaves. I was soaked in light, the blue of the sky, the green of young leaves, the sun shining through them like stained glass. I thought, "When I die, I want to have my ashes buried under this tree, so that for one spring after another my body can be part of this particular green." I could feel my life flowing through the cells of a leaf, feel the leaf opening to the warmth and the light, feel myself part of that green, and I was happy. If that is my afterlife, I will be deeply happy.

The hope of that afterlife doesn't take any leap of faith. I know it can happen. The minerals and the water in my body can be soaked up through the roots of that tree. A part of my body will be unfurling, green in the sun. My soul may be somewhere else. Sometimes I think my soul will float in an ocean of love. Will I recognize old friends, family who have gone on ahead? I don't know. I think I will know they are there. I will know this: there is not now nor was there ever any separation between us. I will know that they were with me as strongly when I was alive as when I'm part of the leaves. The green of a new leaf, lit from behind with the spring sun — that color stays inside me, a glowing place of peace, the certainty of remaining part of life. During a memorial service I see that green, I feel that peace.

This poem by my friend Mary Feagan might be one of my new religion's hymns:

Beauty First

Listen! I learned something this morning.
Fruit comes from flowers. Do you see?
Results come from joy and beauty first.
You don't hammer seeds in the ground
and hope for breakfast.
The important step is in-between.
You eagerly plant ten seeds or a thousand.
Then the seeds, quietly and invisibly
in comfort and heat, drowning and dryness
well, the seeds either die or open up.
And if they open up, if in their own time
they graciously come up for you
what do they do first? You know.
They bloom! "Beauty first!" they shout.
Beauty first, then breakfast.

Haunted by the Sun

ॐ

The pretty yellow flower didn't start pretty. It started as a seed buried in the soil, and its journey, long before blossoming, is already courageous and astonishing. When it's in the dark, not knowing what to do, sleepy and shivering, does it know that the time spent buried is necessary, that the damp and the cold, the time under the ground works toward the moment of breaking open. Something inside the seed is gathering, green, growing as the outside is breaking down. The moment the inside is too strong for the outside, it will break open and the shoot inside starts seeking the sunlight. Antoine St. Exupery says "The seed, haunted by the sun, never fails to find its way between the stones in the ground." The soil around the shoot is pushed aside. If it encounters a stone, and the stone won't be moved, it will grow around the stone, still and always toward the sun. Contemplating this drive in the seed, I wonder what sun haunts me and my growing. Toward what am I always moving? What feeds me, what draws me, what warms and nourishes my life? I think it is Truth. I'm always trying to say the truest thing. My spirit leaps when I hear someone say something true.

What sun draws you toward it? This is a good question for my new religion to offer. It would have been useful information to know early on that I would have to spend some time in darkness, unable to move, not knowing what is coming, and that after that I would break open. I should have been told that the dark is as sacred as the light, a time of resting and attending to the roots.

The religion of my childhood taught that "the heart is deceitful above all things," so you would never be encouraged to follow you heart. I wish I had been assured when I was young that there was something inside me that would guide me, that would fight for expression, find its way past obstacles, feel its way through times of sacred dark. I wish I'd known that there was something inside that would emerge into the light.

I root my experience of aging in what feels to me like the greatest miracle. When the flower is old, its attractive beauty has faded and fallen. What is left is the generative beauty of its seeds, holding within them infinite future plants, infinite flowers, infinite years of beauty and generous giving. This miracle cries out for worship.

The seeds then fall to the ground, or they're carried off by the wind, eaten by birds and dropped miles away. The pretty yellow flower is a traveler, and does not confine itself to blooming where it's planted, despite that cute sign in your Great-Aunt Cordelia's kitchen.

In my religion, anyone being sworn in to public office, would do so with their hand resting on a packet of seeds.

Acknowledgements

ॐ

I've been writing this book for a long time, in bits and pieces. I'm grateful to my readers, who made good suggestions, some of which I took to heart. I'll forever be indebted to my friend, writer Mary Jo Cartledgehayes, who told me that anything less than the truth was going to be boring, and that I didn't have to come up with a good moral for every story. Amy and Bruce Kent did hard work transcribing a week's worth of keynote speeches which were the beginnings of this book. Melanie Taylor found typos and extra spaces, so when you find some, know that they happened because I just wanted to write one more thing into the story that wasn't there when she read it. Gratitude to Susu, Karen, and Dede, my sons and their people, and always to Kiya, with immense love and admiration.

CPSIA information can be obtained
at www.ICGtesting.com
Printed in the USA
BVHW030154171122
652188BV00011B/255